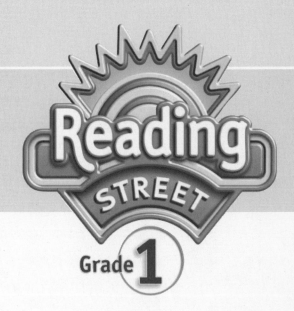

Grade 1

Scott Foresman
Read Aloud
Anthology

Scott Foresman
is an imprint of

Glenview, Illinois • Boston, Massachusetts • Chandler, Arizona
Upper Saddle River, New Jersey

Contents

Ready, Set, Read! My World

Unit 1 Animals Tame and Wild

Unit 2 Communities

Unit 3 Changes

Unit 4 Treasures

Unit 5 Great Ideas

Go Sleep in Your Own Bed

BY CANDACE FLEMING

Pig felt tired. It was time for bed. He headed to his sty, *joggety-jog*. But when Pig lay down, who do you think he found? It was Cow, sleeping soundly in the mud.

"Get up!" squealed Pig, shaking Cow wide awake. "Go sleep in your own bed!"

"So sorry," Cow yawned. "I didn't mean to sleep so long." And she headed to her stall, *clumpety-clump*. But when Cow lay down, who do you think she found? It was Hen, snoring loudly in the straw.

"Get up!" mooed Cow, shaking Hen wide awake. "Go sleep in your own bed!"

"Forgive me," Hen yawned. "I'll move quietly along." And she headed to her coop, *peckety-peck*. But when Hen lay down, who do you think she found? It was Dog, dreaming warm in the roost.

"Get up!" clucked Hen, shaking Dog wide awake. "Go sleep in your own bed!"

"Oops," Dog yawned. "O.K. Good-bye. I'm gone." And he headed for his kennel, *waggedy-wag*. But when Dog lay down, who do you think he found? It was Cat, napping cozy on the rug.

"Get up!" woofed Dog, shaking Cat wide awake. "Go and sleep in your bed!"

"My mistake," Cat yawned. "Do forgive me, drooly one." And she headed to her loft, *pattery-pat*. But when Cat lay down, who do you think she found? It was the farmer, nodding off in the haystack.

"Get up!" mewed Cat, shaking the farmer wide awake. "Go and sleep in your bed!"

"Oh dear," the farmer yawned. "I've been napping way too long!" And she headed to her bed, *quickety-quick*. But when she lay down, who do you think she found?

"Surprise!" hollered Molly, popping out of the covers. "Do I have to go and sleep in my own bed?"

Said her mother with a smile, "Yes, Molly, you have a nice warm bed with lots of stuffed animals waiting for you. Come on, I'll tuck you in!"

Lazy Day

BY EILEEN SPINELLI

One fine day Mama woke up long after the alarm clock went off. "Today is Lazy Day!" she declared.

So breakfast was berries and bananas, and nobody cooked.

We all left our bowls in the sink and went outside where there was plenty to look at.

For the rest of the morning we took it easy and did nothing but look.

Daddy looked at the shed that needed painting. But nobody paints on Lazy Day. So he watched the squirrels instead. They were scurrying around the yard looking for something good to eat.

Grandma looked at the weeds sprouting in her flower garden. But nobody pulls weeds on Lazy Day. So she watched the butterflies instead. They were dancing above the petunias.

Grandpa looked at his dusty red truck that needed washing. But nobody washes trucks on Lazy Day. So he watched Mrs. Albert's pet duck chase the mail carrier and got quite a giggle.

Mama watched our cat stalking a sunbeam.

I watched the sky. Two ship-shaped clouds floated by.

Lazy Day lunch was a picnic in the backyard with chunks of cheese and hunks of bread, and nobody cooked.

After lunch Mama felt like singing. So she did.

Daddy felt like smelling the roses. So he did.

Grandma felt like taking a nap.

Grandpa felt like taking off his shoes and socks.

"Lazy Day" by Eileen Spinelli from *Highlights*, June 2006, Vol. 61, No. 6, Issue No. 656. Copyright © 2006 by Highlights for Children, Inc. Columbus, Ohio. Reprinted by permission.

I felt like splashing in an old garden tub. So I did.

Dinner on Lazy Day was cold leftovers on paper plates, and nobody cooked.

After dinner there was plenty to entertain us. Fireflies and moonrise. Bats against the starlight. Owls hooting. Crickets chirping. Bullfrogs croaking. Neighbors waving and joking about us lazybones lolling in rocking chairs.

But that's how it is on Lazy Day. You don't have to do a thing. You just have to be.

Jenna's Party

BY CASS O'KEEFE

Jenna woke up bright and early, just as the sun was starting to peek into her window. Today was her birthday, and she couldn't wait for her party. It felt great to be seven! This afternoon her favorite people were coming to help her celebrate her special day.

"Mama, who is coming to my party this afternoon?" Jenna asked at breakfast.

"I'm not sure, Jenna," her mom replied. "This is a busy weekend for a lot of people. I didn't hear from Aunt Ginny and Uncle Peter, and your cousin Marty has a big swim meet this afternoon. . . . I guess we'll just see who shows up." Jenna and her mom lived in a not-very-large townhouse with a yard just the right size for a birthday party. Jenna couldn't wait for the fun to begin.

All morning Jenna and her mom worked hard to get the yard ready for the party. Jenna helped blow up balloons and string them around the patio. She set out chairs on the lawn and placed flowers on tables. Finally everything was ready to go. In the yard, a huge colorful banner read "Happy Birthday Jenna!" It was 1:00 and time for the party to begin. Then it was 1:15 . . . then it was 1:30. Where was everybody? "Oh, Mama," Jenna cried, "I guess it's just too busy a weekend for everybody."

Suddenly a car pulled up in front. Out jumped Jenna's cousin Marty and three of his friends from the swim team.

"Hey, I couldn't swim without first wishing a happy birthday to my favorite cousin!" Marty said.

Jenna's Grandma and Grandpa were right behind Marty, with three more of Jenna's cousins. "Sorry we're late. Juana could not find her shoes."

Then came Aunt Ginny and Uncle Peter with more of Jenna's cousins. Mr. and Mrs. Marquez, who lived down the street, stopped by right before Jenna's best friend, Emily, arrived. Before long the yard was filled to overflowing. Jenna's mom opened the patio door so people could move inside for more room.

All afternoon, Jenna played games and ate and opened lots of presents. And then everyone went home, and it was quiet. "Mama, that was the best birthday ever!" Jenna said. "Can we do it again next year?"

My Puppy Sings the Blues

BY ERIN BERGER

Ar-arooooooooo! Chester's sad howl fills the room. Chester is our new puppy. He's only six months old, but his howl is louder than the song I am playing on the piano. He points his puppy head up so high that I can see the white fur on his chin.

Ar-arooooooooo! He howls.

"Chester, this is a happy song," I say. "How about a happy bark?"

I begin playing "Mary Had a Little Lamb" again.

Ar-arooooooooo!

Chester howls every time I practice the piano. He also howls when he sees squirrels outside our living-room window. He howls when I leave the house. He howls when the mail carrier comes. In fact, he howls all the time.

It is always a long, sad howl. His howl sounds like crying. I wonder what makes him so sad.

"Come on, Chester. Let's take a walk," I say.

Chester has been at our house a week, and he already knows what the word "walk" means. Chester wags his tail and licks my hand.

I tell Mom we're going to walk around the block. Then I get Chester's leash out of the closet. He wags his tail even harder.

When we get to the porch, Chester sees a bird on our bird feeder.

Ar-arooooooooo! He howls. He must not like birds.

We walk down the street and see my neighbor Mrs. Grant in her yard. She is playing with her dog, Friskie.

Ruff-ruff-ruff-ruff-ruff, says Friskie. He has a silly bark. It sounds like laughing.

Ar-aroooooooo! Chester says sadly. He must not like Friskie.

Down the block, Mr. Rodriguez is walking with his dog, Pepper.

Yip-yip-yip-yip, says Pepper. She has a cheery bark. It sounds like a ringing telephone.

Ar-arooooooooo! Chester howls. He must not like Pepper either.

We're nearly home again when I see a moving van in front of the house where Mr. and Mrs. Jackson used to live. They moved away a month ago, along with their dog Nellie.

Ar-arooooooooo, says a dog, but it's not Chester. The howl is much deeper than Chester's.

I see a dog come from behind the moving van, along with a girl.

Ar-arooooooooo, Chester howls in his high puppy voice.

The girl waves, so Chester and I walk over.

"Hi! I'm Laura, and this is Jessie," she says, pointing to her dog. He looks just like Chester but bigger. "You have a beagle, too, huh? Don't you love his howl?"

I look down at Chester. His eyes are wide. His tail is wagging. He doesn't look unhappy. Maybe his howl is just his way of saying hello and good-bye and everything else.

"Yes, I do love his howl," I say. "By the way, I'm Autumn, and this is Chester."

Chester and Jessie point their heads to the sky. Ar-arooooooooo!

Show-and-Tell

BY JACK PRELUTSKY

Benny brought a lizard
For show-and-tell today.
He didn't watch it closely,
And the lizard got away.
Carlotta stood and held a plant
That blossomed in a pot.
"I planted it myself," she said.
"I like my plant a lot."

Tim then showed some lightning bugs
He kept inside a jar.
Each one twinkled brightly,
Like a miniature star.
Felice showed off her hamsters,
Named Penelope and Spot.
"These are my hamsters," said Felice.
"I like them a lot."

Amanda had a bird's nest
That she found beneath a tree.
Denise displayed her teddy bears,
I counted twenty-three.
Pete brought in some rope and tied
A complicated knot.
"It's fun to do," he told us.
"I like tying knots a lot."

"Show-and-Tell" from *What A Day It Was At School* by Jack Prelutsky.
Used by permission of HarperCollins Publishers.

I meant to bring my yo-yos,
But I guess that I forgot.
I spotted Benny's lizard
Perched atop Carlotta's pot.
I snatched it in a second,
Though I might have taken less—
Everyone applauded me,
I was a great success.

Market to Market to Market

In the middle of the night, the city market is busy. Trucks, trains, planes, and boats deliver tons of food from farms and fisheries all over the world. Soon owners of grocery stores and restaurants come to buy the fresh fruits, vegetables, and fish. It takes a lot of food to feed a city of hungry people!

Market workers unload the trucks using forklifts. Fruits and vegetables are displayed so buyers can see how fresh the produce is. *Brr!* It gets cold unloading all that food in the dark of night. A fire helps market workers stay warm.

Big scales weigh a lot of little fish. Buyers check over their fruits and vegetables. Each needs to know he got everything his restaurant needs. Some buyers choose fish from the ocean. Then the seller adds up the cost and writes out a bill.

From the market to the grocery store – by morning, fresh fruits, vegetables, and fish are ready for you and your family.

Sometimes farmers sell their produce at farmers' markets. They drive into town while it is still dark, to be ready for early morning customers. Shopping at a farmers' market is almost like going to a party! You can find just the right bag of grapefruit to take home for breakfast.

Just Fur Fun

BY J. PATRICK LEWIS

I set him on my elbow,
I put him on my knee,
I pet him with my finger—
My gerbil tickles me!

I know when he is hungry,
I feed him bits of seed,
And after dinner, there's a book
He likes to hear me read.

Hedgehog

BY HEIDI ROEMER

Racing 'round his squeaky wheel
my hedgehog wakes me up.
I offer him a mealworm snack
and fill his water cup.

Wispy bits of cedar chips
cling to him—to me.
I stroke his spiked pincushion back
so so gingerly.

He's never learned to fetch or heel
or answer when I call.
Instead, he climbs my welcome hand
to snuggle in a ball.

The Storm Seal

BY JUDY WAITE

The weather was wild. Angry lightning scratched across the grumbling sky. The waves heaved and hurled. In the exploding night, pressed against giant gray rocks, the seals were huddling.

By morning, the storm had faded. The wind dropped to a shout, then a whisper. Along the sand an old man was walking, clearing trash. And as he searched carefully among piles of seaweed, something stirred.

Tangled in the knots of an old fishing line lay a tiny seal pup, barely breathing. "Poor little thing," said the old man, wrapping it gently in his sweater.

A boy playing on the beach spotted the old man. "It's Peter!" he cried, calling out to his friends. "I think he's found something." The retired sailor was well-known in the village for rescuing hurt animals.

Peter put his fingers to his lips as the children came near. "Shhh," he whispered gently. "Don't crowd around. He needs lots of peace and quiet." The children understood, and watched silently as Peter carried his precious bundle up the steep path to his home.

Peter made a place in his kitchen for the baby seal and offered him fish soup from a bottle. But the little pup just closed his eyes and turned away. So Peter sat and stroked his head and sang to him softly all the songs he knew from his days at sea.

By evening, the pup had taken his first spluttering drink. And when the soup was gone, he sucked gently on Peter's hand for comfort, while the velvet night crept softly in through the windows.

The next morning, the little seal seemed brighter. And as the days passed, he grew stronger still. Soon, he had lost his white baby fur and was eating the fresh fish Peter tossed to him every morning.

He often followed Peter around, and when the days grew warmer, he played in the garden with the other animals.

Now that the seal was better, the children came to visit him. He rolled on his back and pawed them with his flipper, like a dog wanting a game.

More and more people came to see the little seal. Peter was glad they were interested. But he was also thankful when the night came and the two of them could enjoy the quiet for a while.

Then, one morning, Peter fell ill. The doctor came and ordered him to bed. But Peter was anxious about all his animals. "Don't worry," the doctor said. "I'll arrange for someone to help."

And he did. The local people were wonderful. They shopped and they cleaned, they brushed and they fed. Every day after school, the children came. They helped with all the animals, but most of all, they loved to help with the seal.

One day, the children brought a ball and taught the seal to balance it on his nose. They dressed him up in sunglasses, a hat, and a scarf. The seal looked funny in his new outfit, but he didn't look much like a seal any more.

Upstairs, Peter was feeling better. He wondered what all the noise was about. Slowly, he got up and went downstairs.

Nobody noticed him as he stood in the doorway. They were all too busy laughing at the seal. "Oh no," said Peter, stepping forward. "Remember, he's a wild animal. He might nip if he gets frightened. And he's much too special for tricks and toys." Peter knew now that he had something to get strong for.

Early each morning, Peter rowed out to sea. He took the seal along, and taught him how to dive for food among the silver flashes of fish.

One morning, as the soft pink of sunrise still washed the sky, Peter saw something moving around the rocks. It was a great colony of seals. One seal broke away from the others, and swam right up to the boat. Peter's seal stared hard at the stranger. "Don't worry," said Peter gently. "It's a friend."

The seal touched Peter lightly with his nose, then leaped into the water with a splash of sparkling silver. The other seal swam with him, nudging and nuzzling him, then dived suddenly away.

Peter's seal swam back to the boat. "It's all right," said Peter. "It's time for you to go." Then Peter's seal dived after his new friend, and the game began.

The two seals raced and chased, they rumbled and tumbled, deep in the water under the boat. And Peter rowed back to the shore through the bright burst of morning.

On the beach, the children were waiting. They were worried about the seal. "Look out to sea," said Peter, pointing. "He's back where he belongs."

The children turned to see two black shapes bobbing and splashing in the water. "He has a friend already," said Peter, smiling. "And see, it looks like they're laughing. It looks like they're happy." As they watched the seals slip away into the distance, Peter and the children were happy too.

Paul Bunyan and Babe

A Traditional Tall Tale

This is the story of Paul Bunyan. Now, this is no ordinary story. It's an American legend. Legends are favorite stories that people have been telling each other for hundreds of years. They tell about great heroes and their glorious adventures. Now, these adventures are not exactly true, but they are based on real people and places from history.

So, who was this legendary hero, Paul Bunyan? Paul was a lumberjack who lived back when the United States was a very young nation with many thick and wild forests everywhere. Lumberjacks cut down trees to make lumber for building houses. But Paul Bunyan was no ordinary lumberjack. No sir. He was so huge, he was bigger than life. And strong? Oh my yes. The legends say that Paul could cut down the tallest, fattest trees with a single swing of his mighty ax!

Paul Bunyan was even born big. How big? His mother would rock him in a cradle that was the size of a grownup's bed, that's how big. And Paul grew bigger and bigger in a hurry. No normal clothes would fit him. His mother had to make all Paul's clothes, and on his shirts she used wagon wheels for buttons!

Now, an enormous and powerful man like Paul needs an enormous and powerful pet, don't you think? So Paul got himself a pet ox that was as big as he was! A big blue ox he named Babe. Blue? That's right—a big blue ox.

How did Paul find this enormous blue ox? Well, one day during the Winter of Blue Snow, Paul came across a baby ox who had fallen into a stream. He rescued this calf from drowning, named him Babe, and raised and cared for him. Like Paul, Babe grew very big very fast.

How big did Babe grow? The legends say it took a crow an entire day to fly from the tip of one horn to the other. Imagine that! And Babe was a big eater too. A very big eater. For a snack, the blue ox would eat thirty bales of hay—wires and all! Paul took real good care of Babe too. He used a pine tree to brush Babe's hair and clean Babe's teeth. Before long, Babe was full-grown with a body so powerful that he could pull and push anything, even mountains! Anything except Paul, that is. Nothing on Earth was powerful enough to push Paul Bunyan, not even Babe the blue ox.

Paul and Babe made a terrific team. Together they changed the land of the whole United States. Paul and Babe cleared acres and acres of trees from North and South Dakota. Farmers followed close behind them, planting crops on the newly cleared ground. And soon, waving fields of golden wheat and yellow corn covered the land.

Paul and Babe built roads too. One time, Paul used Babe to straighten a crooked road.

Now, that road was thirty miles long to begin with, but by the time Babe was through straightening that road out, it was twelve miles longer! That was OK, though. Paul just rolled up those extra twelve miles of road and gave them back to the town to use somewhere else.

Paul and Babe worked together in the forests too. Paul would chop down the trees and Babe would drag them out into a nearby lake or river. Then those logs would float along across the lake or down the river to a sawmill, where other men would pull the logs out of the water and saw them into boards.

Paul thought of a great idea to make logging easier. He dug the Puget Sound out of the Pacific Ocean on the coast of Washington state to make a waterway for getting logs to the mill. And that wasn't all the digging he did. You've heard of the Grand Canyon, that great big canyon thousands of people visit each year? Well, do you know where it came from? That's right. Paul and Babe dug it out of the Arizona earth. And Paul also dug out the five Great Lakes. He did it as a favor to Babe. You see, the enormous blue ox needed a water dish.

Lakes, canyons, plains, and roads—Paul and Babe shaped them all. Or did they? Were these American heroes real or make-believe? What do you think?

Takhi

BY KAREN MAGNUSON BEIL

A mother horse chases after her frisky baby here on the grassy Mongolian plain. This baby is special. She is *wild!*

When she grows up, she won't look exactly like the tame horses we know. Her kind of horse, the takhi (TAH-kee), are the only true wild horses. For centuries these shy horses roamed the lowlands, birch woods, and mountains of Mongolia and China. Wolves preyed on them. So did a few human hunters. But the horses survived.

Then things got worse for the takhi. Herdsmen moved more and more hungry cattle into the area. The cattle ate the grass that the takhi liked to eat. Finally people and cattle had taken over all the space—there was no more room for the takhi. Once there had been thousands of takhi. By 1970, there were none left in the wild.

Luckily, a few takhi had been captured and were living in zoos around the world. Now some of these beautiful horses are going home to the plains of Mongolia.

STEPS TO FREEDOM

The zoo-born horses had always been fed by people. They didn't know how to survive in the wild. So first the people created six large park-like areas in the Netherlands and Germany (two countries in Europe). Then they gathered some of the takhi from the zoos and put them in these new parks. There, the horses learned how to find their own food.

AND IN MONGOLIA . . .

At the same time, thousands of miles away, Mongolian scientists were busy selecting a wild place for the horses to live. The Hustai Nuruu National Park would be perfect. It would have everything wild horses could need—springs and rivers for water all year, birch woods for shelter from harsh winter winds, and grasses for food. And people living nearby would be happy to herd the takhi back if they wandered away from the reserve.

COMING HOME

In 1992, the first 16 horses were brought from the parks in Europe to Mongolia. They came in wooden crates by airplane. These were young adult horses. The horses were put into groups to create new families. Each group lived in a separate pen for a few days. There, they got to know each other—*howdy!*—and to rest up after their long trip.

Next, they spent many months in a larger area. They got used to living in Mongolia, where the weather is much colder, the water tastes different, and hungry wolves roam nearby. Each move gave the horses more space and freedom—and more challenges.

Once the groups bonded as families, the takhi were released—racing, chasing, galloping—into the reserve. They were free! They were wild! They were home at last!

FOLLOWING A DREAM

Saving the wild horses was the dream of a Netherlands couple, Jan and Inge Bouman, and their friends. Jan had loved horses ever since he was young. As a boy he'd sneak out to the barn at night to sleep with his pet horse.

A few years ago, he and Inge saw some endangered takhi at a Netherlands Zoo. They decided to help return them to their native land.

Right from the start, the Boumans understood something important: If the horses moved into Mongolia, their human neighbors there would be affected. So they worked with the local people, conservation groups, and scientists from all over the world. Together they created new jobs for herdsmen whose cattle could no longer graze in the reserve. They even trained some of the herdsmen to be rangers to keep track of the horses.

The old herdsmen remembered stories about the wild horses. Now, this special wild place is home to the takhi once again. But that's not all. Mongolian gazelles, wolves, foxes, polecats, vultures, and cranes are finding their way back to the protected reserve. These animals teeter on the edge of survival. Maybe this will be their second chance too!

Maisie Caught a Toad Today

BY TRYN PAXTON

Maisie caught a toad today, and she doesn't want to let him go.

She found the toad in the garden, sitting still as a stone in the shade of a zucchini leaf. Maisie put the toad in a bucket with some mud and rocks and zucchini leaves, so he'd feel at home.

"Let him go," said her mother when Maisie showed her the toad. "He'll starve if he doesn't have enough bugs to eat."

"I'll catch one hundred bugs to feed him every day," said Maisie.

"Let him go," said her father when Maisie showed him the toad. "His skin will dry out. He'll get dehydrated."

"I'll sprinkle him with water ten times every day," said Maisie.

Maisie sat and looked at her toad in the bucket. He looked back at her. His throat puffed in and out as he breathed.

Maisie picked up her toad and stroked him with her finger. His skin was bumpy.

Suddenly the toad hopped right out of Maisie's hand. He hopped again and then again until he found a shady spot to rest. There the toad sat still as a stone.

Maisie looked at her toad. She looked in the empty bucket and frowned.

Then Maisie carried the bucket to the garden. She turned it on its side and half buried it in the dark, moist dirt near the zucchini. Maisie decorated the opening of the bucket with a few rocks and leaves. She even made a tiny pond for the toad near the bucket. She lined the pond with pebbles and filled it with water from the garden hose. Now the toad's home was ready.

Maisie picked up her toad, still sitting in the shady spot where she had left him. Maisie placed the toad near the opening of the bucket. The toad hopped in and sat still as a stone inside his shady new home. He looked at Maisie. His throat puffed in and out as he breathed. Maisie looked back at her toad and smiled.

When Animals Are Doctors

BY DEBORAH CHURCHMAN

USING MEDICINE

If you get sick or hurt, a doctor may treat you and give you medicine to help you get better. Animals don't have doctors. But some kinds "doctor" themselves.

Chimpanzees eat a lot of leaves and other plant parts. Some have been seen swallowing bristly leaves whole. As the leaves pass through a chimp's body, they act a bit like a broom, "sweeping out" worms and other pests that could make the animal sick.

A chimp can find a leaf from an aloe plant and break it open. It can smear liquid from the leaf over a sore on its foot. It may just use the leaf to wipe off the sore. But some people use aloe to treat burns and scrapes. So perhaps the chimp does that too.

HAVE YOU HAD YOUR CLAY TODAY?

Ripe fruit is delicious. Many, many different animals try to nab it. Unripe fruit and seeds are often poisonous. Eating them makes most animals very sick, so few animals eat them.

Red-and-green macaws have a neat trick. This trick lets them eat the unripe foods that grow where they live along the Amazon River. After eating the poisonous food, the birds find some clay to eat. The clay mixes with the poisons in their stomachs and keeps the poison from doing any harm.

MONKEYING AROUND

Red colobus monkeys have a different way to protect their stomachs. These monkeys live on the African island of Zanzibar. Growing there are Indian almond, mango, and other fruit trees. These trees have very bitter leaves that are high in protein. Protein helps to build strong muscles, but the leaves may make the monkeys sick.

The monkeys have a way to solve this problem. During a big leaf meal, the monkeys nibble on charcoal from burnt wood. Scientists think the charcoal mixes with the leaves' bitter acids and helps protect the monkeys' stomachs. Pretty smart, huh?

EAT DIRT

Elephants scoop up gobs of mud to eat. Why? Because the mud contains lots of minerals. Usually, plants provide the minerals that elephants need. But where some live, the plants don't have enough minerals in them to keep the animals healthy. So the elephants have found a goopy way to get them.

BONE UP ON CALCIUM

Giraffes chew on bones to get a mineral called calcium. Rodents, gopher tortoises, and many other animals also nibble on old bones and antlers for the calcium they need.

Scientists are still discovering different tricks that animals use to doctor themselves. They wonder if some of these same tricks and medicines could help people. After all, everyone wants to stay healthy!

100th DAY WORRIES

BY MARGERY CUYLER

Jessica was a worrier. She worried about everything. She worried about losing her first tooth, and remembering her lunch money, and missing the school bus, and getting her math right.

But on the 95th day of first grade, Jessica's teacher gave her something new to worry about.

"Next Friday will be the 100th day of school," Mr. Martin said. "So I want each of you to bring in a collection of 100 things. They can be anything you want, but they should be small, like rubber bands or marbles. We'll display our collections out in the hall."

Immediately Jessica began to worry. "Oh no," she groaned to herself. "What will I bring?"

All weekend long Jessica thought and thought. But each new idea brought new worries with it. 100 ice cubes? Too melty. 100 marshmallows? Too sticky. 100 toothpicks? Too pointy.

That night at dinner, Jessica asked her family for ideas.

"How about 100 yo-yos?" suggested Tom. "Where would I get 100 yo-yos?" asked Jessica.

"Maybe 100 lipsticks would work," said Laura. Jessica rolled here eyes. Laura might have that many tubes of lipstick, but Jessica sure didn't.

"We know you'll think of something," said Mom and Dad. "You have until Friday."

On Monday, the 96th day of school, Jessica watched as Bobby gave Mr. Martin 5 bags of peanuts. "There are 20 peanuts in each bag," Bobby explained.

"Great!" said Mr. Martin.

"Why didn't I think of peanuts?" Jessica wondered.

On the 97th day of school, Jessica watched as Sharon piled paper clips into 10 neat stacks on Mr. Martin's desk. "100 paper clips in all," Sharon announced.

"Wonderful!" said Mr. Martin.

"How did she find so many?" wondered Jessica.

On the 98th day of school, Jessica watched as Ashley brought in 100 peppermints. "I ate a few," she admitted. "So I really only have 95." She promised to bring in 5 more peppermints the next day.

"Fantastic!" said Mr. Martin.

Jessica's stomach felt queasy.

By the time Jessica went to bed on the 99th day of school, she still hadn't thought of anything to bring.

On Friday morning, she sat at the breakfast table and stared at her cereal.

"Jessica?" asked Mom. "What's wrong?"

"Today is the last day to bring in 100 things for the 100th day of school, and I still haven't thought of the right thing," she said. "I've only come up with stuff that's too melty or too sticky or too pointy. I'll be the only kid without anything to show, and everyone will make fun of me."

Jessica began to cry.

"Don't worry," said Dad. "I have an idea!"

He pulled open one of the kitchen drawers. "Here are some ribbons," he said, giving Jessica a handful of scraps.

Jessica counted. 3 red, 2 green, 2 yellow, 2 purple, and 1 striped.

Mom ran down to the cellar and brought back a jar. "Here are some screws," she said, dumping a pile on the table.

Jessica counted. 4 big, 4 small, 1 giant, and 1 tiny.

"Here are some rocket-shaped erasers from my collection," said Tom. "4 pink, 3 green, 2 white, and 1 yellow."

"Here are some beads from my necklace that broke," said Laura. "3 round, 4 oval, 2 square, and 1 shaped like a smiling cat."

"I'll get some buttons from my shirt drawer," said Dad. He found 5 black, 3 brown, and 2 white.

"Here's some loose change from my purse," said Mom. "10 pennies and 10 nickels."

"Here are 10 barrettes I don't need anymore," said Laura.

"How much stuff do we have so far?" asked Mom.

Jessica looked at the stuff on the table. It wasn't 100 of anything, but at least she had something to show. Something was better than nothing.

"There's the bus!" said Mom. "Here's a bag for your things. Don't forget your lunch!"

Jessica shoved everything into the bag and ran to catch the bus.

All morning Jessica thought about the stuff in the bag. She tried to remember the things her family had given her. 10 ribbons, 10 screws, 10 erasers, 10 beads, 10 buttons, 10 pennies, 10 nickels, 10 barrettes, 10 rocks. That came to 90. She needed 10 more! Where could she get 10 more things? Oh no, here came her worries again.

At lunch Jessica found a note in her lunch box.

Sweetie,

We'll help you find more stuff this weekend. I'm sure Mr. Martin will understand if your collection is late.

Don't worry!

Love, Mom XXXXXXXXXX

Suddenly Jessica had a great idea. She smiled to herself as she waited for lunch to be over.

After story hour, Mr. Martin said it was time to put their 100 things out in the hall. "What did you bring, Jessica? he asked.

"Here are 10 ribbons from my dad," she said.

"10?" asked Mr. Martin.

"And 10 screws from my mom," said Jessica.

The other kids came over to look.

"And 10 erasers from my brother and 10 beads from my sister," said Jessica.

"Pretty," said Anita.

"And here are 10 buttons from my father, and 10 pennies and 10 nickels from my mother, and 10 barrettes from my sister, and 10 rocks from my brother's iguana's aquarium," said Jessica.

"Cool," said Leslie.

"And what this?" asked Mr. Martin

"It's 10 kisses from my mom," said Jessica. "See?" Jessica pointed to the 10 Xs written on her mother's note that stood for kisses.

"I brought in 100 things my family gave me," said Jessica. "Is that okay?"

"Wow!" said Mr. Martin. "I've seen a lot of great collections for the 100th day of school, but this one . . ."

Jessica swallowed.

"This one is really special," said Mr. Martin. "You've brought in . . . 100 bits of love!"

Iris and Walter
The School Play

BY ELISSA HADEN GUEST

1. Exciting News

Iris and her best friend, Walter, raced outside after school. They had exciting news to tell Grandpa.

"Our class is putting on a play!" said Iris.

"What's the play about?" asked Grandpa.

"It's about bugs," said Iris.

"I'm going to be a dragonfly," said Walter.

"And I'm going to be a cricket," said Iris. "I have three lines to say, and Walter has three lines too!"

"And Miss Cherry said that after the play we're going to have an ice-cream party," said Walter.

"What fun!" said Grandpa.

That evening, Iris told her parents and Baby Rose all about the play. "Do you want to hear my lines?" she asked.

"Of course," said her mother.

"I can't wait," said her father.

"Quiet, everyone," said Grandpa.

Iris opened her notebook and read:

"I am a cricket. I chirp and hop. My ears are on my front legs."

"Ears on your legs!" said Iris's mother.

"Well, how about that," said Iris's father.

"You'll make a wonderful cricket," said Grandpa.

Iris said her lines at dinner. She said her lines to Baby Rose. And by the time Iris fell asleep, she knew all her lines by heart.

2. Stage Fright

The next day, Miss Cherry said, "This morning you are all going to work on your costumes."

"Oh good," said Walter. Walter loved to paint and draw.

"And while you are working, you can practice your lines." said Miss Cherry.

"Great," said Iris. Iris loved saying her lines.

"Will you help me with my lines, Iris?" asked Walter.

"Sure," said Iris. "Will you help me paint my wings?"

"Of course," said Walter.

Walter helped Iris with her wings. They sparkled in the sunlight. Iris helped Walter with his lines until he knew them perfectly.

All week long, the children practiced their lines. The day before the play, Miss Cherry said, "Today we're having our dress rehearsal on the school stage."

"I've never been on a stage before," said Walter.

"Isn't it exciting?" said Iris.

"Remember to speak your lines slowly," said Miss Cherry. "And use a strong, loud voice. You can go first, Walter."

"Okay," said Walter. Walter cleared his throat. "I . . . ," said Walter.

But suddenly, Walter could not remember his lines.

"I am a dragonfly," whispered Iris. "I have four wings and six legs. I eat mosquitoes."

"I am a dragonfly," said Walter. "I have four wings and six legs. I eat mosquitoes."

"Good," said Miss Cherry. "You just need to practice a little more, Walter. I know you are going to do very well."

But now, Walter was worried. "What if I forget my lines when we do the play?" he whispered to Iris.

"Don't worry," said Iris. "I know your lines. I can whisper them to you."

But Walter was still worried.

3. A Terrible Day

That night, Iris put on her costume for Baby Rose and danced around their room.

"You're coming to the play tomorrow, Rosie!" Iris told her sister.

Baby Rose smiled and said, "Da, Da, Da."

"But you'll have to be very quiet, Rosie," said Iris. "You can't make any noise, okay?"

"Iris, my girl, what are you doing up?" asked Grandpa.

"I'm not sleepy," said Iris. "I can't wait for tomorrow."

"Even crickets need their sleep," said Grandpa. "Now close your eyes, and before you know it, it will be morning."

The next day, Iris woke up very early. Her head hurt. Her throat was sore. Iris was sick!

"Iris, my love," said Iris's mother, "you have to stay in bed today."

"But today is the play!" croaked Iris.

"I know, my Iris," said Iris's father. "But you can't go to school when you have a fever."

"I can't miss the play," wailed Iris. "I can't miss the ice-cream party. And I have to help Walter remember his lines!"

But Iris's parents would not let her go to school. They tucked her into their bed. They brought her tea with honey. They gave her blackberry candies to soothe her throat. Iris cried and cried. After a while, she fell asleep.

Iris slept all day. When she woke up, it was evening. School was over. There was a card on the table.

Dear Iris,

I remembered all my lines.

Get well soon.

Your best friend,

Walter

4. Better Days

On Monday, Iris was well enough to go to school.

"Look, everybody, Iris is back!" said Walter.

Iris felt as if she'd been gone a long time.

"Welcome back," said Miss Cherry.

"It's too bad you had to miss the play," said Benny.

"Everyone clapped a lot," said Jenny.

"The ice-cream party was so much fun!" said Lulu.

Iris felt a lump in her throat. Her nose stung.

"Don't feel sad, Iris," said Walter.

"I missed the play," said Iris. "I missed the ice-cream party. I missed everything."

"I know it's hard," said Miss Cherry. "But there will be other plays, Iris, I promise."

"Later on, I'll have a surprise for everyone," Miss Cherry whispered. "I think you'll enjoy it."

At snack time, Miss Cherry said, "Iris, will you help me pass out the surprise?"

When Iris saw the surprise, she started to laugh. There were green-frosted dragonfly cookies and orange-and-yellow butterfly cookies. There were cricket and ant and ladybug cookies.

"How do you like my bug cookies?" asked Miss Cherry.

"They're beautiful," said Benny.

"They're delicious," said Iris.

"I'm glad," said Miss Cherry. "Now I'll tell you what we are going to study next."

On the way home from school, Iris and Walter had exciting news to tell Grandpa.

"Our class is going to put on a dance!" said Iris.

"It's about the solar system," said Walter. "I'm going to be Mars."

"And I'm going to be the Sun," said Iris.

"You'll both be splendid," said Grandpa.

And they were.

How a City Grows

Long ago, where there's a big city now, there were once just meadows, and hills, and forests. What happened?

Like a person, a city starts out small—and grows.

At first there were just a few houses or farms. There were no roads, just trails that deer or other animals followed. People traveled by horse or even canoe. But mainly they walked wherever they needed to go.

As more people came, some built their own farms. Others opened small stores. Some people became carpenters or blacksmiths. Others were workers who built houses, washed laundry, unloaded ships, or drove carts.

As the town grew, railroads and factories came—along with even more people looking for jobs. There are no cities without jobs for people to do to earn money for their families. With more families, the town needed schools and libraries and newspapers and banks. The city grew and grew.

Finally, the city was huge! Millions of people lived and worked in tall skyscrapers. The streets were crowded with cars and buses and trains. There were large, fancy stores and theaters and sports stadiums. Underground pipes brought water from the lake to the buildings, and wires carried electricity.

Now the city is very busy—and very exciting!

"How a City Grows". Reprinted by permission of Cricket Magazine Group, Carus Publishing Company, from *Click* magazine, May/June 2003, Vol. 6, No. 5, English text copyright © 2003 by Carus Publishing Company.

Grandma Elephant's in Charge

BY MARTIN JENKINS

Most elephants live in families. And most elephant families are **big** (just like elephants). There'll probably be two or three babies, forever playing push-me-pull-you, or peekaboo, or anything else that makes a lot of noise. And each of the babies might have an older brother or sister—handy for playing king-of-the-mountain on! And then there are the moms. They take care of their own babies and help with one another's too—keeping an eye on them to make sure they don't wander off, and scolding them when they get too boisterous. But that's not all. The most important member of an elephant family is . . .

Grandma!

Grandma's been around a long time and she knows lots of important things. She knows where the water holes are when it hasn't rained and the easiest places to cross the big river when it has rained. She knows where to find the juiciest melons . . . And knows the best path up the cliff to the salt lick. It's not surprising that she's the one in charge.

She doesn't make a big song and dance about it, though. Just a flick of the ear or a snort or two, and a **rumble, rumble, rumble,** deep down in her throat, seem to be enough to tell all the other elephants what to do.

If she stops, they all stop. If she moves, they all move. And if there's any sign of danger, you can be sure she'll be the first to investigate and the first to decide what the family should do. They might all run away or they might take a stand. Or Grandma might **c-h-a-r-g-e.**

If she charges with her head up and ears flapping, waving her trunk and making a great hullabaloo, then she's probably bluffing. But if her head's down, her trunk's tucked under, and she's not making any noise, then she means business. In that case, whoever it is that has annoyed her had better watch out.

And once all the commotion's over, everyone can settle back down to feeding and snoozing and messing around—knowing that Grandma has sorted things out again. So if you're an elephant, there's one thing you should never forget. Wherever you are and whatever you're doing, **Grandma's in charge!**

Why Beavers Love Wolves

BY GERRY BISHOP

It's easy to imagine why wolves would "love" beavers—they think they're delicious! But why in the world should beavers love wolves?

Many years ago in what is now Yellowstone National Park, the mountain valleys were filled with beavers. The beavers had built dams of sticks and mud across the mountain streams, and quiet ponds had formed behind the dams.

The ponds were safe places for the beavers to build their lodges. Good thing too, because gray wolves prowled nearby, and they were always happy to catch a fat beaver for dinner.

The ponds—and the bushes and trees that grew around them—were also good homes for many other kinds of wildlife. Large deer called elk sometimes came to find food there. But they spent most of their time far away in thick forests where they could more easily hide from the hungry wolves.

But then human settlers came to this wonderful place, and they killed off all the wolves.

Why? Because they feared and hated wolves and because they thought they were doing good by getting rid of them. But with no wolves around, some no-good things began to happen.

There were no wolves to chase them, so the elk started hanging out around the ponds as long as they liked. Now they ate as much of the trees and bushes as they wanted.

That meant that soon the beavers couldn't find enough food for themselves. They also had no branches for building dams and lodges. So they left or died.

With no beavers to repair them, the dams on the old beaver ponds broke. The ponds disappeared, and rushing water cut deep, muddy gullies in the soil. Here few plants could grow and few animals could live.

And what about the elk? They wandered off to the places where they had lived in the days of the wolves. But they never forgot about the food they had found around the old beaver ponds.

Every spring, the few trees and bushes that still grew there sprouted new leaves and twigs. And every spring, the elk came back to gobble them up.

Finally, people captured some wolves in far-off places and brought them back to Yellowstone. The wolves started catching and eating the elk, just as they had done so many years before. The wolf packs grew in number, and they ate more and more of the elk.

The elk that survived still came to feed where the old beaver ponds once were. But they didn't stay very long for fear of the wolves. Soon the bushes and trees began growing back.

Before long, beavers returned and began building dams again. The dams held back the rushing water, and new ponds began to form. Other animals that needed the ponds came back too. Yes, there were now fewer elk, but there were far more creatures of other kinds.

The beavers had to watch out for hungry wolves, of course—just as they had before. And sometimes the wolves would catch one for dinner. But now the beavers had plenty of food and safe places to hide. And that's the way it would stay for a long time to come.

That's why beavers—and many other kinds of wildlife—should love wolves.

The Ant Parade

BY MARILYN L. SLOVAK

"Come on. Let's go!" Annie Ant shouted to her brothers and sisters who were scurrying about on the anthill.

"Hurry up. Don't want to be late!" Arnie Ant called down the tunnel to all his relatives underground.

Ants poured out of the hill. The oldest of the ants, Auntie Lulu, told everyone what to do. "Form a single file. March quickly and in a straight line. Don't wander off and get lost in the tall grass or flowers."

As all the ants got in line, the air filled with their excited voices.

"Do what Auntie Lulu says."

"Isn't this fun!"

"Stay in line."

"Have you ever done this before?"

"Don't wander off into the daffodils."

"What a treat."

"I can hardly wait!"

Following closely, one behind the other, the ants filed down the hill and into the grass. Auntie Lulu, marching at the head of the line, started to sing in time to their stamping feet.

> "Marching, marching,
> One, two, three;
> Busy, happy
> Ants are we."

Soon all the ants were singing along with Auntie.

"Marching, marching,
One, two, three;
Busy, happy
Ants are we."

The long parade of ants marched and sang its way through the tall grass, past the maple tree, and around the daffodil patch. They followed Auntie Lulu as she led them across a slab of cement and up the leg of a wooden table.

"We're here," said Auntie Lulu. "Let's get to work. We'll start at the top. Youngest ants first. Annie and Arnie, you lead the way for your brothers and sisters."

Eagerly the young ants climbed to the top of a large, brown, sticky object in the middle of the table. Each took a piece and crawled back down. By the time all the sister and brother ants had taken a bit, the older ants did not have very far to climb.

"All right, everybody." Auntie Lulu was giving orders again. "Let's go home."

The ants lined up behind Auntie Lulu. Each ant carried a large, gooey, sugary chunk. They began their march back to the anthill—down the wooden table leg, across the slab of cement, into the grass, around the daffodil patch, past the maple tree—singing all the way.

"Marching, marching,
One, two, three;
Busy, happy
Ants are we."

Mrs. Jacobs stepped out of the back door of her house and onto her patio.

"Oh no!" she cried. "What has happened to my beautiful chocolate cake? I set it on the picnic table to cool, and now there are only a few crumbs left."

As the last of the smiling ants disappeared down the tunnel into the anthill, a new song echoed through their underground home.

"Lunching, munching,
Ants are we;
Full and happy,
Yes, sirree!"

Out in the Country

BY JUDY PEDERSEN

When I was very small, we moved from our Brooklyn apartment to a quiet little New England town.

My grandparents had given us land.

"Get of the city," they'd said, "and build yourselves a house in the country."

And that's just what we decided to do.

At first we lived in a makeshift cabin on a large pond.

A sappy peach tree grew alongside the pond.

When the warm, fuzzy peaches were ripe, my grandmother and I made peach preserves.

Willowy, silver birches and wild blackberry bushes grew in our backyard, and a cool, clear creek followed the edge of our yard to a beaver dam, then tumbled over into another pond and the deep woods.

One morning, as the sun rose above the trees, we began work on our new house.

Between a tall black locust and a spindly white ash, my father drove a long pine stake into the ground.

I was the north corner, and my brother was the south.

One by one, we measure the corners of our house in the grass.

"Building a house takes a long time," my mother told us, "and we'll need help."

My uncles piled rocks—flat, round, and squarish—in rows to make a foundation.

The men framed our house with long planks of good-smelling spruce.

And when they were finished, we could see the clouds and stars through the openings.

Bit by bit, they began to close the house in with walls.

A bricklayer built a chimney and then we had a large open fireplace.

Before long, our house needed a roof.

Hundreds and hundreds of little cedar shingles wove our house a hat.

And in the autumn, at the end of a long sunny day, when the days had become shorter and the night had become longer, our house was finally finished.

Hermia's Shell

BY BISH DENHAM

Hermia the hermit crab wanted a new shell. Her old black-and-white whelk was getting a bit tight.

"I want a special shell," she said to her friend Henry. "I want a shell that's pink inside and creamy outside with chocolate brown stripes. When we get to the beach," Hermia added, "I'm not going to settle for just any old black-and-white whelk. I want a shell that says something about *me*."

Henry grunted as he rolled down the side of the hill.

When they arrived at the beach, thousands of hermit crabs were swapping news—and shells.

Hermia passed up many shells that would have fit her just right.

"That one has a chip on the lip," she said to Henry. "And see how this one's been faded by the sun? Just look at that one, it's all worn along the bottom. I wouldn't live in it if it were the last shell on the beach!"

One by one, all the hermit crabs left the beach, returning to their homes high in the hills. Even Henry had long since said good-bye.

When she was about to give up, Hermia found it. There, being gently washed by the lapping waves, was a beautiful apple murex. It was pink inside and creamy outside with chocolate brown stripes.

When she tried it on, it was much too big. It flopped and wobbled so badly, she kept falling over onto her back. Then she had to wiggle her legs madly to right herself. Hermia knew she'd

"Hermia's Shell" by Bish Denham from *Spider Magazine, August 2006, Vol. 13, No 8.* Copyright ©2006, Carus Publishing Company.

never make it back into the hills, so she decided to live by the beach.

It was a long, lonely year. By the time the hermit crabs returned the next summer, Hermia had finally grown into her new shell.

"See my new shell?" she said to every crab that came her way. "See my beautiful apple murex? It's pink inside and creamy outside with chocolate brown stripes. I had to spend the whole year all by myself because it was too big. But now I've grown into it, so I can go back into the hills with you."

Hermia found Henry and traveled with him.

"I'm so excited about my new shell," she said. "I want to show it to everyone. Have you noticed its lovely ridges and how gracefully it spirals to a perfect, unbroken tip?"

Henry groaned as he fell into a hole and struggled to climb out.

All Hermia could talk about was her shell. The other hermit crabs started to avoid her and began to talk about her behind her shell.

Even Henry got tired of her. "Hermia," he said, "if you say one more thing about that shell, I'm going to find another hill to live on."

"But it's so unique!" she exclaimed. "I think you're jealous."

Henry shook his feelers and crawled away.

Hermia crawled off in the opposite direction. "I'll just find new friends who will appreciate me," she said.

When she met new hermit crabs, they soon got bored with her, too.

"They'd steal my shell if they could," she said to herself.

In time, Hermia began to feel her shell getting tight. At first she ignored the pain where her soft abdomen curled into the tip of the murex. By the time of the summer migration, Hermia was moving very slowly. Still, when she got to the beach, all she could talk about was her shell.

None of the crabs wanted to hear it.

"You're all jealous!" Hermia replied, limping away angrily. "You're just waiting for me to swap it so you can fight over it!"

Hermia was in so much pain, she could barely move. She knew it was time to find a new home. But all she found was a black-and-white striped whelk shell.

"How common," she thought. But she knew she had to make the move.

Hermia tried to get out of her shell. She pulled and pulled, but she was stuck. And oh! It hurt so much, she could hardly stand it. Finally, there was a little sucking noise and a *pop!* Hermia tumbled out of her beautiful apple murex.

The pink inside had turned a dull gray. The creamy outside with the chocolate brown stripes had faded to white. The fine ridges and lip were chipped and cracked. The very tip of the spiral was broken off. The bottom was worn smooth.

In horror, Hermia realized she'd been dragging around and bragging about a very worn and battered shell.

Hermia slipped into the whelk. Its smooth mother-of-pearl interior was cool and soothing to her poor, pinched abdomen.

When she returned to the hills, no one recognized her. When they found out who she was, they were surprised. Even Henry began to talk to her again, because now they could have real conversations about things that mattered.

"Henry, I've made a decision," said Hermia. "Next summer I'm going to help the younger crabs find good homes."

"I can hear it already," Henry said. "'If the shell fits, wear it!'"

Hermia laughed. It felt good.

Pup Grows Up

BY SUSAN YODER ACKERMAN

On a rocky shore by the gray ocean, Sandy, a newborn harbor seal, is crying. His mother calls back to him. They touch noses.

The mother nudges her big-eyed pup. She wants him to swim with her. They flop and wriggle their bodies toward the water's edge.

Sandy follows his mother right into the water. He's not afraid. Without any lessons, he can already swim and knows how to hold his breath underwater.

Sandy and his mother have fun splashing through the water or floating lazily around on the waves.

Though his tiny teeth are already sharp, Sandy won't be eating any fish yet. He's still too little. But he watches curiously as his mother catches and eats a herring. Before long, he'll learn to dive and hunt like she does.

Soon Sandy will grow a thick layer of fat to keep him warm in the cold water.

For now, his mother takes him back to shore, where he lies down on the rocks and gets warm in the sun. After all, he's still a little pup.

But he grows bigger as the days go by. He starts to nibble the crabs and shrimp he catches with his mother. And, like all the other seals, he rests on the sun-warmed rocks when he's tired.

"Pup Grows Up" by Susan Yoder Ackerman from *Zootles, November/ December 2007, Volume 2 Issue 6.* Copyright © 2007 Wildlife Education, LTD®.

One afternoon, when Sandy is a few weeks old, he wakes up hungry. He looks all around him, but his mother isn't there. He cries for her, waiting for her call, but all he hears are the cries of other pups nearby and the cries of gulls wheeling in the sky. *Where can she be?* the pup worries, and cries again.

Suddenly, his mother's smooth head pops out of the water. She hears him! Her large dark eyes look for her pup. She wiggles her nose to catch his smell. He cries one more time, and this time she calls back. She sees him. She flops across the rocks and they touch noses once again. To Sandy, his mother smells just right, and he smells just right to her, too.

Soon Sandy will be old enough to spend the day with other seal pups, without his mother nearby. Soon he'll go out fishing on his own. But for today, he snuggles close to his mother and knows that all is well.

Jack and the Beanstalk

A TRADITIONAL TALE
ADAPTED BY RON FRIDELL

Once upon a time in England, there lived a poor woman and her son, Jack. They were so poor they had to sell their belongings to get enough food to eat. Finally, all they had left was a cow. "Go to the market in town and sell the cow—and make sure you get a good price," she told him. So Jack set off to market with the cow.

On the way, he met a merchant who said he would trade a handful of magic beans for the cow. Jack wanted the beans. So he made the trade, tucked the beans into his pocket, and dashed home as fast as he could. "Look, Mother, magic beans!" he cried.

But Jack's mother was not at all happy with the trade her son had made. "What good are a handful of beans?" she wailed. "What will we do now? We have no food. We have nothing," she said. But Jack planted the beans in the garden anyhow and went to bed wondering what wondrous things would grow from them.

The next morning, Jack saw that the beans were special indeed. For overnight, a humongous beanstalk had grown exactly where Jack had planted the beans. The leafy green stalk stretched clear to the sky and into the clouds. "I bet I'll find food up there," Jack told his mother.

"Be careful," she said as he started climbing.

Jack climbed and climbed until he reached the clouds. When he climbed through them and into the light again, he was at the top of the beanstalk. And there was a huge castle with a dozen tall towers and a hundred gleaming windows.

Jack hurried in and sure enough, there was food in the castle, more food than he had ever seen in his whole life! But there was also a humongous giant sitting down to eat all that food. Suddenly the giant stood back up and sniffed the air and peered all around and pounded the table with his massive fist, shaking all the castle's hundred windows. "Fee-fi-fo-fum. I smell an Englishman!" he shouted.

Jack crouched in a corner trembling, wondering if the giant would find him. When the giant gave up and ate his food, Jack sighed with relief. Then the giant took a goose from a golden cage. Jack watched in amazement as it laid a golden egg at the giant's feet. The egg gleamed as the giant picked it up and held it to the light. After a while, the giant fell asleep, and Jack bravely grabbed the goose, ran from the castle, and climbed back down the beanstalk.

Back at home, Jack's mother told him that once she and his father had owned a goose like this—and more. But a giant had taken all of their things! Now Jack was determined to get back everything that the giant had taken from his family.

The next day, he climbed the beanstalk again. As Jack tiptoed into the castle, he saw the giant sitting down to eat again, and again the giant cried out, "Fee-fi-fo-fum. I smell an Englishman!"

Jack hid again, trembling, until the giant finished eating. Then the giant brought out two bags of gold, set them at his feet, and eyed them greedily. When the giant finally fell asleep, Jack grabbed the gold, climbed down the beanstalk, and returned the stolen gold to his mother.

The next day, Jack climbed the beanstalk once more. And once more Jack hid in the corner as the giant sniffed the air and cried out, "Fee-fi-fo-fum. I smell an Englishman!" But once again Jack hid and the giant could not find him. This time, after his dinner, the giant brought out a magic harp, which played soothing music that soon put the giant to sleep.

Jack saw his chance, grabbed the harp, and ran. But the magic harp cried out, "Help!" and woke the giant, who came running after Jack. As Jack rushed down the beanstalk, he called to his mother to get him the ax. He would have to destroy the beanstalk before the giant reached the ground. With all his might, Jack chopped and chopped until down came the beanstalk. And down with it came the giant, striking the earth with a giant thud!

Jack's mother was thrilled to have Jack and all their belongings back. With their goose, their gold, and their magic harp, Jack and his mother never had to worry about being hungry again. They ate well and lived happily ever after.

Song of the Cicada

BY TRISTIN TOOHILL

Late in the summer, on a cool evening, Addy and her father heard a song high in the trees. "Listen!" said Daddy. "Cicadas!"

Together they searched the trees around their yard and found empty cicada shells. "An insect used to live inside," Daddy explained. "When it grew bigger, it left its shell behind." Gently Addy and Daddy pulled the fragile shells off the trees and collected them in a bucket.

Just as Addy reached for one of the shells, it began to walk! The cicada was still inside. Addy watched it slowly crawl up the tree. Then it stopped and sat motionless for what seemed like a long time. A small crack began to open down its shell. The crack got wider and wider, until Addy could see the insect's back emerging. When its head popped out, Addy looked right into its shiny green eyes.

Slowly and gently each leg slipped out the shell–two small ones on the front, two in the middle, and two bigger ones on the back. Addy could see two tiny thin wings that looked like wet paper.

Daddy brought out a chair. "Aren't your legs getting tired?" he asked. "You've been watching for almost an hour now."

"Look, Daddy!" exclaimed Addy. "Something is happening to the wings."

"The cicada has tiny vessels in its wings," said Daddy. "It fills these vessels with fluid from its body to expand the wings."

Patiently Addy sat in her chair and watched and watched. The sun went down, and the air became very cool. Mommy called from the house, "Time to come inside!"

Reluctantly Addy went inside. When she was ready for bed, she and Daddy took his flashlight out to check on the cidada once more. It was still resting on its shell.

"It was hard work for the cidada to come out of its shell," said Daddy. "It probably needs a long rest."

When Addy woke the next morning, she ran outside to the tree to check her cicada. A fragile, dull, empty shell was hanging in the spot she had stared at for so long.

That evening, as Daddy pushed Addy on her swing, they heard a familiar song high in the trees.

"Listen!" said Addy. "My cicada!"

Busy Busy Moose

BY NANCY VAN LAAN

Fall

There was a chill in the air. Moose could see his breath. He looked up. The leaves were gold and red and brown.

"It must be fall," said Moose. "I will go tell Beaver."

"Hello, Beaver," said Moose. "Do you know what season it is?"

"Yes," said Beaver. "It is fall."

"How did you guess?" asked Moose.

"I can see my breath," said Beaver. "The leaves are gold and red and brown."

"Oh," said Moose. "We both saw the same things."

"And," said Beaver, "this is the busiest time of the year."

"Why?" asked Moose

"I have to make my winter house," said Beaver.

Moose went to see Squirrel.

"Hello, Squirrel," said Moose. "Do you know what season it is?"

"It is fall," said Squirrel. "I can see my breath."

"Me, too!" said Moose.

"This is my busiest time of the year," said Squirrel. "I have to hide acorns."

Moose went to see Rabbit. Rabbit also knew it was fall. He was busy too. He was busy gathering bark and twigs.

Moose did not need a house. He did not need to gather acorns or bark and twigs. He did not need to gather anything at all. Moose had nothing busy to do.

He walked into the middle of a great wide field. There he stood for a long time, all alone. A flock of birds flew by. They were on their way south for the winter.

One tiny bird landed on Moose's antler. Then another. And another. Soon Moose's antlers were full of birds. He did not know they were there.

Rabbit hopped by. "You look very busy," he said.

"Busy?" said Moose. "Busy doing what?"

"Busy being a tree," said Rabbit. "Your antlers are full of birds."

Moose looked surprised.

"You are a perfect resting spot," said Rabbit, and he hopped off.

Oh, thought Moose. *I must stand very still. This will be my job.*

Each day Moose stood in the field. Each day a new flock of birds flew by. Each day his antlers were full of birds. Now fall was the busiest time of the year for Moose too.

Winter

"Halloo, Moose!" Beaver called. "Come see my new winter home!"

Moose waded all the way to the other side of the pond. He stuck his big nose through the small front door.

"What a fine home," said Moose.

"Please don't come in," said Beaver. "You are too big."

"HALLOOOO!"

It was Rabbit. He was on the other side of the pond.

"Come see my new home," called Beaver.

But the water was too deep. Moose waded over to Rabbit.

"Hop on," said Moose.

Moose took Rabbit across the deep pond.

"Come in, Rabbit," said Beaver.

"Your home is so warm and dry," said Rabbit.

Moose poked his big wet nose inside.

Hmmm, thought Moose.

"HALLOOOO!"

It was Squirrel.

"Come see my new home," said Beaver.

But the water was too deep.

"Here I come," said Moose.

"You are a perfect ferry boat," said Squirrel.

"Come in," said Beaver to Squirrel.

"Your home is just the right size," said Squirrel.

Moose poked his big nose inside.

Hmmm, thought Moose.

"HALLOOOO!" said Mouse

So Moose carried Mouse to Beaver's new home, too.

Beaver, Rabbit, Squirrel, and Mouse sat inside, warm and dry. Only Moose's nose was warm and dry. The rest of him was not.

It was time to say goodbye.

"Please come again soon," said Beaver.

"We shall!" said Rabbit, Squirrel, and Mouse.

They hopped onto Moose. Back across the pond they went.

Beaver watched Moose cross the pond again. Poor Moose! How weary he must be.

That month, Beaver had lots of visitors. Each day, Moose was a ferry boat. He was tired of this job. But he did not quit.

One bitterly cold day, the pond froze. No water. Just thick ice.

Hooray!" said Moose.

Now Rabbit, Squirrel, and Mouse hopped across—all by themselves. And Moose could rest.

Spring

It was spring. The birds were nesting. It was their busiest time of the year. Moose was busy being himself.

One day while Moose was napping, a baby bird fell out of its nest. Guess where it landed?

The mama bird flew round and round. She fussed and fussed. Moose woke up. He thought she was admiring his new antlers.

Along came Beaver.

"You have a houseguest," said Beaver.

"I do?" said Moose.

Moose walked to the pond. He looked at his reflection.

"Oh, my!" said Moose. "Last fall I was the perfect resting spot."

"Now," said Beaver, "you are a perfect *nesting* spot."

But when Moose tried to walk again, the mama bird flew round his head. She fussed and fussed. She screeched in his ear: *Trees don't walk!*

Moose tipped his head to the right. The baby bird hopped to his right antler. He tipped his head to the left. The baby bird hopped to his left antler. He tipped his head all the way back. The baby bird landed on his nose. That tickled Moose.

"AHHHHHHH-CHOOOOOO!"

Away went the baby bird. He could fly!

"Now you can just be Moose again," said Beaver.

"Good," said Moose. "In the spring, being just a moose is what I do best.

Summer

It was a hot summer day. Moose was grazing in the meadow. He did not look busy. But he was. Moose was busy thinking: *Summer is a time for thinking good thoughts. It is a time to dream. A time to plan.*

Beaver was floating in his pond. He did not look busy. But he was. Beaver was busy thinking: *Summer is a time for thinking good thoughts. It is a time to dream. A time to plan.*

Moose dreamed of winter. He saw himself busy being a ferry boat.

Beaver dreamed of winter too. He saw himself in his warm, dry house.

Suddenly, Beaver had an idea.

Moose had an idea too.

That night, while Beaver slept, Moose got busy. He rolled rocks, lots of big rocks, down to the creek.

The next day, while Moose was in the meadow, Beaver got busy. He swam back and forth, his mouth full of sticks.

At the end of the day Moose went to see Beaver. They always spent the end of each day together. They liked to take turns talking. Today Moose went first.

"I have a surprise for you, Beaver."

"Oh," said Beaver. "I have a surprise for you too."

"Follow me," said Moose. "You can *walk* on my surprise."

Moose crossed the creek on the rocks. So did Beaver.

"Now," said Moose, "you can have visitors all winter long!"

Then Moose snorted. "Beaver, where is your house?"

"Oh, Moose!" said Beaver. "That was my surprise for you!"

Beaver pointed. His new home was now on the other side of the pond. Moose and Beaver laughed and laughed.

Beaver hopped on Moose's back. Together they went to see Beaver's new winter home. This time, it was large enough to fit half a moose inside.

Fall Again

There was a chill in the air. Moose could see his breath. He looked up. The leaves were gold and red and brown.

"Hooray!" said Moose "It's fall again."

He walked into the middle of the great wide field . . .

. . . and waited.

Treasures of the Heart

BY ALICE ANN MILLER

Come along with me to see,

the greatest treasure that will ever be.

It's not in chests on pirate ships

or in your favorite birthday wish.

It's buried deep and very safe.

I have it in my special place.

Come along, it's through this door.

Crawl with me along the floor.

We're getting closer. Watch your head.

Yes! Here it is, beneath my bed.

A paper clip, a potato chip, a broken pen, and three toy men.

Don't move the fuzz!

It's there because it helps me hide the loot!

Let's see . . .

A coffee can a rubber bank and . . .

YUK! . . . Oh, never mind.

A yellow sock, my lucky rock, let's see what YOU can find.

My favorite car, my cricket jar, a two-year-old bird's nest.

A peach pit, one pointed stick.

What do you mean?

"This is a mess!"

For everything that's under here,

There's a story I could tell.

I've collected all these treasures

and I've kept them very well.

When I couldn't save the whole,

I stored away a part.

Everything you see here

is a treasure of my heart.

No one but you has ever seen

the wonders I've just shared.

The paper planes, some dried up rain, and genuine

rabbit hair.

I wanted you to see my stuff

and have fun with it, too.

You wouldn't want to break my heart and throw

it out . . .

Mom? Would you?

Princess Clarabelle

BY ELIZABETH PASSARELLI

Being a princess is hard work, thought Princess Clarabelle as she tried to sit up straight on her small and not very comfortable royal throne and watched a group of musicians play. Her mother and father, the king and queen, sat beside her and smiled politely as they listened to the lively tune.

Princess Clarabelle looked longingly at the big drum and wished she could play it. She tapped her foot to the beat. Her mother put a gentle hand on her knee to remind her that princesses don't tap their royal feet. Princess Clarabelle sighed.

When the music ended, Princess Clarabelle clapped along with the rest of the royal court. The musicians grinned broadly, and she grinned back.

"Clarabelle," her mother whispered in her ear, "princesses do not grin."

Clarabelle tried to smile politely, but a giggle bubbled up inside her and escaped. Her mother sighed.

That evening when the queen came to kiss her good night, Princess Clarabelle asked, "Mama, may I please learn to play an instrument?"

"Of course, my dear. I'll have the music master begin giving you lute lessons tomorrow," her mother answered.

"But Mama, I don't want to play the lute. I want to play the drums," Clarabelle said.

"Clarabelle, princesses don't play drums."

"Why not?

"It's not princess-like," the queen said.

The next day, Princess Clarabelle and the queen took their daily walk in the royal garden. They admired all the royal roses and the royal lilies and the royal pansies. Clarabelle watched the royal gardener's children as they played ring-around-the-rosey until they all fell laughing on the grass. Clarabelle laughed, too, while the queen smiled.

"Mama, let's play ring-around-the-rosey!" Clarabelle begged.

"Clarabelle, princesses don't fall on the grass," the queen answered gently. "I'm sorry."

"Princesses don't get to do anything," Clarabelle grumbled.

As she took her bath that evening, Clarabelle splashed and dunked in her royal bathtub, pretending to be a dolphin leaping through the waves. She remembered the time she went with her mother and father to watch the royal ships come in. Clarabelle had seen people diving and swimming in the sparkling blue sea. She'd picked up a seashell and slipped it into her pocket to take home.

Once Clarabelle was in her royal nightgown, she opened her box of treasures and took out the seashell. She touched the shell's smooth inside and tried to peer into its spirals.

When the queen came in to kiss her good night, Clarabelle asked, "Mama, can I go swimming in the ocean?"

"Oh, Clarabelle," her mother answered.

"Princesses don't go swimming?" Clarabelle asked.

The queen shook her head. "I'm afraid not." Her eyes were sad. "I always wanted to swim, too."

Clarabelle ran and got her shell from her box of treasures.

She held it up to her mother's ear.

"Can you hear the sea?" she asked.

As the queen listened, her eyes grew wide with surprise. Then she laughed and gave Clarabelle a hug.

"Mama, what were you like when you were a princess?"

"Just like you, Clarabelle." Her mother smiled and kissed her good night.

The next morning, Princess Clarabelle was not in her royal bed. When the queen finally found her in the royal library, Clarabelle was searching the shelves.

"I can't find it," Clarabelle said.

"What are you looking for?" asked her mother.

"The book of rules for princesses," said Clarabelle.

"There is no book of rules, Clarabelle," the queen told her.

"Then where did they come from?" Clarabelle asked.

"I don't know," the queen said, thinking hard.

Clarabelle had an idea. "Why don't we write our own book of rules?" She grinned broadly.

The queen grinned back. "Why not?"

They sat down side by side at the royal desk and wrote rule number one: A princess may play the drums!

The Statue of Liberty

BY SHEILA KEENAN

She has stood tall over New York City's harbor for more than 100 years. When she was young, she was a warm copper brown. Steamships chugged past her, bringing millions of immigrants to America, their new home. Now she's a pale green. The boats still come, but they are ferries bringing millions of visitors to her feet.

The Statue of Liberty is an immigrant herself! She was made in France. The French people gave her to the United States to celebrate democracy. Frédéric-Auguste Bartholdi, a French sculptor, designed the statue he called "Liberty Enlightening the World" in 1870. Some people say the statue is modeled after his mother's face and his wife's body.

The Statue of Liberty proudly holds a torch with a golden flame in her right hand. In her left hand, Liberty holds a tablet with July 4, 1776, the date of the Declaration of Independence, carved on it in Roman numerals. She wears a crown with seven spikes in honor of the seven seas and the seven continents. There's a broken chain under her feet, which stands for America's independence.

Bartholdi's Liberty is enormous . . . and hollow! The sculptor used a special method to create a copper "skin" that gives the statue its shape. More than 300 sheets of copper were hammered over the statue model.

These metal sheets were only 3/32 inch thick, about as wide as a rubber band! They gave the Statue of Liberty its shape. But what was going to hold up its 62,000 pounds of copper skin? A "skeleton," of course.

Bartholdi contacted Alexandre-Gustave Eiffel, a brilliant French engineer. (He would later build the famous Eiffel Tower in Paris.) Eiffel designed an iron skeleton of four tall iron beams with cross braces.

Eiffel's ironwork skeleton was built in Paris. It rose 984 feet high. There was a double spiral staircase in the middle: 162 stairs up, 162 stairs down. (That's still how you get up to the Liberty's crown—step by step!)

By 1884, the astonishing statue was finished. The Statue of Liberty loomed over Paris. At a ceremony on July 4, 1884, Bartholdi and the French government officially gave the statue to the United States. Now, it had to get there.

The Statue of Liberty was carefully taken apart. Every copper piece and iron bar was labeled. The 350 pieces were packed in 214 crates and shipped to New York City. The ship docked in June 1885, but the crates stayed packed. There was nowhere to put the statue yet!

The French expected the Americans to build a pedestal, or base, for the Statue of Liberty. But not enough Americans had given money to build this base. Joseph Pulitzer, an immigrant who had become a successful publisher, was outraged. Pulitzer wrote about the problem in his newspaper, the *World*.

He also printed the name of anyone who gave money—even a penny—for the pedestal.

Nickels, dimes, and dollars poured in. Even children gave. In five months, 121,000 people sent $102,066.39. The pedestal builders went to work. By April 1886, they were finished. Then it took several more months to rebuild the statue on her pedestal.

Finally, on October 28, 1886, the Statue of Liberty was unveiled. Bartholdi pulled off the French flag covering her face. Cannons roared. Ship whistles tooted. Crowds cheered.

Lady Liberty was home at last!

Gila Monsters Meet You at the Airport

BY MARJORIE WEINMAN SHARMAT

1

I live at 165 East 95th Street, New York City, and I'm going to stay here forever. My mother and father are moving. Out West. They say I have to go too. They say I can't stay here forever.

Out West nobody plays baseball because they're too busy chasing buffaloes. And there's cactus everywhere you look. But if you don't look, you have to stand up just as soon as you sit down. Out West it takes fifteen minutes just to say hello. Like this: H-O-W-W-W-D-Y, P-A-A-A-R-D-N-E-R. Out West I'll look silly all the time. I'll have to wear chaps and spurs and a bandanna and a hat so big that nobody can find me underneath it. And I'll have to ride a horse to school every day and I don't know how. Out West everybody grows up to be a sheriff. I want to be a subway driver.

My best friend is Seymour, and we like to eat salami sandwiches together. Out West I probably won't have any friends, but if I do, they'll be named Tex or Slim, and we'll eat chili and beans for breakfast. And lunch. And dinner. While I miss Seymour and salami.

2

I'm on my way. Out West. It's cool in the airplane. The desert is so hot you can collapse, and then the buzzards circle overhead, but no one rescues you because it's real life and not the movies. There are clouds out the window. No buzzards yet.

I'm looking at a map. Before, whenever I looked at a map, I always knew my house was on the right. But no more. Now I'm in a plane above the middle of that map, and I'm going left, left. Out West.

Seymour says there are Gila monsters and horned toads out West, and I read it in a book so I know it's so. But Seymour says they meet you at the airport.

3

We're here. Out West. I don't know what a Gila monster or a horned toad looks like but I don't think I see any at the airport.

I see a boy in a cowboy hat. He looks like Seymour, but I know his name is Tex. "Hi" I say.

"Hi," he says. "I'm moving East."

"Great!" I say.

"*Great?*" he says. "What's so great about it? In the East it snows and blows all the time, except for five minutes when it's spring and summer. They ran out of extra space in the East a long time ago. It's so crowded people sit on top of each other when they ride to work. And alligators live in the sewers. I read it in a book so I know it's so."

Then the mother and father of the boy who looks like Seymour but isn't grab his hand, and he goes off. "Sometimes the alligators get out," he yells to me. "And they wait for you at the airport."

4

It's warm, but there's a nice breeze. We're in a taxi riding to our new house. No horses yet. I don't see any buffalo stampedes either. I see a restaurant just like the one in my old neighborhood. I see some kids playing baseball. I see a horse. Hey, that's a great-looking horse! I'm going to ask my mother and father for one like it.

Here's our house. Some kids are riding their bikes in front of it. I hope one of them is named Slim.

Tomorrow I'm writing a long letter to Seymour. I'll tell him I'm sending it by pony express. Seymour will believe me. Back East they don't know much about us Westerners.

The Talking Cloth

BY RHONDA MITCHELL

Aunt Phoebe has things. Things and things and things. "A collector of life," Mom calls her.

I like visiting Aunt Phoebe. There's no place in her house to be bored, and she always gives me mocha to drink. Daddy says it will stunt my growth. Aunt Phoebe tells him, "Mocha is named after a city in Yemen, and this child just grew an inch or two, *inside*, for knowing that."

Aunt Phoebe knows things . . . She tells me stories, about her "collection of life," each time we visit. I sip hot mocha and listen, imagining all the people and places she has seen.

Today we sit in her kitchen and she tells about the basket of folded cloths in the corner. "I bought these in Africa," she says.

Aunt Phoebe smiles and takes a cloth from the top of the basket. She unfolds it with a flourish—a long magic carpet. It runs like a white river across the floor.

"What do you do with such a long cloth?" I ask.

"You wear it," says Aunt Phoebe. "It tells how you are feeling. This cloth talks."

"How can it do that?"

"By its color and what the symbols mean," Aunt Phoebe tells me. "This is *adinkra* cloth from Ghana. It's made by the Ashanti people and at one time only royalty wore it," she says. Aunt Phoebe rubs the cloth against my face.

It's silk and feels smooth. I imagine myself an Ashanti princess....

The cloth is embroidered in sections and hand printed all over with small black symbols. Like words. A white cloth means joy—yellow, gold or riches. Green stands for newness and growth. Blue is a sign of love, but red is worn only for sad times, like funerals or during wars.

Aunt Phoebe tells the meaning of some symbols on her cloth. Each symbol speaks of something different, like faith, power or love.

I imagine cloths with my own symbols on them. Fred— he's my little brother—should be dressed in green for "go" with grubby little handprints all over. Everyone can see what kind of a mess that kid is.

Aunt Phoebe's little brother is my daddy. "Let's see," she says. "Guess we could wrap him in gray pinstripe cloth for seriousness, with squares on it!" We all laugh, imagining that.

I ask if I can put on the *adinkra* cloth. "Of course you can, baby," Aunt Phoebe says. "When you're older, you can have it for your own." She wraps the *adinkra* three times around my waist, then across one shoulder—and still it drags on the ground.

"A cloth this long is a sign of wealth," she tells me.

Daddy says, "Amber, you'll need to drink a lot of mocha to grow tall enough."

"Well," says Aunt Phoebe, "this child has grown a lot, *inside*, just today!"

I smile, thinking of it. This cloth means joy. I am an Ashanti princess now, and here is all my family and everyone who has ever worn an *adinkra* . . . gathered around me.

The Unbeatable Bread

BY LYN LITTLEFIELD HOOPES

One dark morning
still dreaming in bed,
Uncle Jon sat up and said,
"I will bake an unbeatable bread."

"Bread?" sighed Aunt Lucy, "Oh, dread!"

"A wild bread," said Uncle Jon.
"A wishing bread
as bright as dawn…"

His wife gave a tremendous yawn.

"Uncle Jon,
the children are grown.
We've no one to eat it,
no nieces or nephews or cousins to knead it!
No grammas, no grampas,
no good great-aunts…"

Uncle Jon pulled on his pants.

"I will bake an unbeatable bread.
I'll wake the world from winter's sleep,
melt the snow, the dark so deep;
I'll break the spell of this long freeze,
bring out the children and the honeybees."

Aunt Lucy gave a substantial sneeze.

"Uncle Jon, you've baked enough.
The kitchen is full of poofs and puffs,
cookies and crumb cakes with chocolately chips..."

Uncle Jon just licked his lips.

"I will bake an unbeatable bread,
an undefeatable bread!
A YES bread, make-a-mess bread,
a LOUD bread, feed-a crowd bread..."

Aunt Lucy sat straight up and said,
"Mr. Makin' Bread, Mr. Muffin Head,
if we've no one to eat it,
and we're snowed in tight,
you'll be the one to eat every last bite.
Now stop your bakin',
pack up your pans,
stop eatin' the dough
off your hands,
stop clanging your spoons,
singing your songs,
banging about with your bing bang bongs…"

"I'm bakin' a bread,"
sang Uncle Jon,
"a wakin' bread.
I'm bakin' a shakin' wakin' bread."

Aunt Lucy pulled the pillow over her head.
She knew there'd be no one
to eat that bread.

Uncle skipped to the kitchen
stuffed with poofs and puffs,
pulled out the bread pans
and all the bread stuffs,
and as he worked,
he hummed along,
singing his wakin' bakin' song.

"I'm bakin' a bread,
a wakin' bakin bread,
bakin' a shakin' wakin' bread."

He mixed in the yellow
of the morning sun,
a whistle in the wind,
clouds on the run.

The bread dough rose
as he sang along.
He rolled it in a loaf,
and it wasn't long
'til the smell of bread baking
rose up with his song.

It floated upstairs
and along the halls,
slid out the iced windows
through cold, damp walls.
It sailed over trees all robed in white,
wrapped 'round houses
snowed in tight.

The sweet wheaty smell
seeped under doors,
rose softly ringing
through cracks in floors.

It floated by firesides
in sleepy dogs' yawns,
played in fiddles
and old French horns,
slipped into hats,
mufflers, and mittens,
wrapped around alley cats
and little skinny kittens.

Now, alone by the window
Uncle watched the snow,
blowing deep, drifting slow;
and as he watched, he hummed along,
whisipered his wakin' bakin' song.

"I'm bakin' a bread,
a wakin' bread,
bakin' a shakin' wakin' bread."

The sweet smell roamed
over snowy billows
and great white hills
like giant pillows.
It blew into bear caves
and foxes' dens,
woke rabbits and moles
and sleeping wrens.

It whispered 'round snowmen
stooped under trees,
and whistled in hives of honeybees,
rose into bedrooms,
rumbled in snores,
and crept with the spiders over nursery doors.

"A wakin' bread,
a shakin' bread,
bakin' a shakin' wakin' bread…"
Uncle scrubbed up as he sang along,
and the smell of bread baking
sailed on with his song.

It floated over bumps
and little lump-lumps;
it pooled in quilts,
and climbed mountainous rumps.

Then silently, secretly by it slid,
and found them each
under pillows hid.
Emma and Mia,
Liza, Sam, Miss Boo,
on it went to find Stevie too.

OFF with the blankets!
OFF-OFF with the spreads!
OFF with the sheets
on the winter white beds!

The smell of bread
reached down deep,
lifted them each out of sleep,
and waking them
with dreams of spring,
it wafted them off on great soft wings.

The sea sang silver,
and the skinny mooned smiled
as they sailed away the morning miles,
and the gray sky ran to gold and red
with the perfect browning of the bread.

Now here was the sun,
up and coming,
and here was Stevie,
hum-hum-humming.
And a tap on the window,
two, three, four,
Emma and Mia
rapping on the door.

"Makin' a bread,
a bread so fine..."
Uncle Jon sang in the big sunshine.

"Bakin' a bread,
a bread so true!"
There was Liza and Sam and old Miss Boo.

"Bakin' a bread,
a bread so proud!"
Up flew the bees in a soft brown cloud.
"Bakin' a bread,
a bread so good!"

In came the creatures
from the wood,
rabbits and moles
and singing wrens,
foxes and bears hungry from their dens.

"Bakin' a bread,
an *undefeatable* bread!"
Aunt Lucy woke to the sun overhead,
popped off her pillow to smell that bread.

"Baking a bread,
an *unbeatable* bread!"
Aunt Lucy tiptoed out of bed,
and snuck downstairs to see that bread.
Uncle Jon swung wide the kitchen door,

and in they came, dripping on the floor,
gathered 'round and ready, waiting to be fed
a great big bite of the unbeatable bread.

Pancake Party

A SIBERIAN FOLK TALE

Little Mouse, Raven, and Snowbird lived together in a
cozy little tent on the tundra.
They cooperated very well . . . . most of the time.

One morning Little Mouse woke up thinking of pancakes.
"Let's make pancakes today."
"I love pancakes!" said Raven.
"Me too!" said Snowbird.

"Who will go to town to buy the flour?"
"Not me," said Raven. "I'm too busy."
"Not me," said Snowbird. "I'm too busy."

"Then I'll go myself," said Little Mouse.

And she did.

Little Mouse pulled her sled down to the store.
She bought the flour.
She pulled her sled back home again.

"Here is the flour.
Now who will mix the batter?"

"Pancake Party" from *Three-Minute Tales: Stories from Around the World to Tell
or Read When Time is Short* by Margaret Read MacDonald. Copyright © 2004
Margaret Read MacDonald. Published by August House Publishers, Inc. and
reprinted by permission of Marian Reiner on their behalf.

"Then I'll mix it myself," said Little Mouse.

And she did.

Little Mouse put in the flour.
She put in egg.
She put in water.
She stirred that batter until it was smooth.

"The batter is ready.
Now who will fry the pancakes?"

"Not me," said Raven. "I'm still busy."
"Not me," said Snowbird. "I told you I was busy."

"Then I'll fry them myself," said Little Mouse.

And she did.

Little Mouse made her griddle very hot.
She poured batter on her griddle.
She flipped the pancakes over and fried them on both sides.
Soon she had a pile of pancakes all ready to eat.

"The pancakes are ready.
Now who will eat the pancakes?"
"I will!" said Raven.
"I will!" said Snowbird.

"Oh no, you won't," said Little Mouse.
"You watched while I went for the flour.
You watched while I mixed the batter.
You watched while I fried the pancakes.
So you can watch while I eat them!"

And they did.

She sat right down and ate those pancakes up . . .
every one.

And since the pancakes are finished . . . well, so is
this story.

Bread and Jam for Frances

BY RUSSELL HOBAN

It was breakfast time, and everyone was at the table. Father was eating his egg. Mother was eating her egg. Gloria was sitting in a high chair and eating her egg too. Frances was eating bread and jam.

"What a lovely egg!" said Father. "If there is one thing I am fond of for breakfast, it is a soft-boiled egg."

"Yes," said Mother, spooning up egg for the baby, "it is just the thing to start the day off right."

"Ah!" said Gloria, and ate up her egg.

Frances did not eat her egg. She sang a little song to it. She sang the song very softly:

> I do not like the way you slide,
> I do not like you soft inside,
> I do not like you lots of ways,
> And I could do for many days
> Without eggs.

"What did you say, Frances?" asked Father.

"Nothing," said Frances, spreading jam on another slice of bread.

"Why do you keep eating bread and jam," asked Father, "when you have a lovely soft-boiled egg?"

"One of the reasons I like bread and jam," said Frances, "is that it does not slide off your spoon in a funny way."

"Well, of course," said Father, "not everyone is fond of soft-boiled eggs for breakfast. But there are other kinds of eggs. There are sunny-side-up and sunny-side-down eggs."

"Yes," said Frances. "But sunny-side-up eggs lie on the plate and look up at you in a funny way. And sunny-side-down eggs just lie on their stomachs and wait."

"What about scrambled eggs?" said Father.

"Scrambled eggs fall off the fork and roll under the table," said Frances.

"I think it is time for you to go to school now," said Mother.

Frances picked up her books, her lunch box, and her skipping rope. Then she kissed Mother and Father good-by and went to the bus stop. While she waited for the bus she skipped and sang:

> Jam on biscuits, jam on toast,
> Jam is the thing that I like most.
> Jam is sticky, jam is sweet,
> Jam is tasty, jam's a treat—
> Raspberry, strawberry, gooseberry,
> I'm very FOND . . . OF . . . JAM!

That evening for dinner Mother cooked breaded veal cutlets, with string beans and baked potatoes.

"Ah!" said Father. "What is there handsomer on a plate and tastier to eat than breaded veal cutlet!"

"It is a nice dish, isn't it?" said Mother. "Eat up the string-bean, Gloria."

"Oh!" said Gloria, and ate it up. She had already eaten her dinner of strained beef and sweet potatoes, but she liked to practice with a string bean when she could.

"Where do breaded veal cutlets come from?" asked Frances. "And why are French-cut stringless beans called *string* beans?"

"We can talk about that another time," said Father. "Now it is time to eat our dinner."

Frances looked at her plate and sang:

> *What do cutlets wear before they're breaded?*
> *Flannel nightgowns? Cowboy boots?*
> *Furry jackets? Sailor suits?*

Then she spread jam on a slice of bread and took a bite.

"She won't try *anything* new," said Mother and Father. "She just eats bread and jam."

"How do you know what you'll like if you won't even try anything?" asked Father.

"Well," said Frances, "there are many different things to eat, and they taste many different ways. But when I have bread and jam I always know what I am getting, and I am always pleased."

"You try new things in your school lunches," said Mother. "Today I gave you a chicken-salad sandwich."

"There, now!" said Father to Frances. "Wasn't it good?"

"Well," said Frances, "I traded it to Albert."

"For what?" said Father.

"Bread and jam," said Frances.

The next morning at breakfast Father sat down and said, "Now I call that a pretty sight! Fresh orange juice and poached eggs on toast. There's a proper breakfast for you!"

"Thank you for saying so," said Mother. "Poached eggs on toast *do* have a cheery look, I think."

Frances began to sing a poached-egg song:

> *Poached eggs on toast, why do you shiver*
> *With such a funny little quiver?*

Then she looked down and saw that she did not have a poached egg. "I have no poached egg," said Frances. "I have nothing but orange juice."

"I know," said Mother.

"Why is that?" said Frances. "Everybody else has a poached egg. Even Gloria has a poached egg, and she is nothing but a baby."

"But you do not like eggs," said Mother, "and that is why I did not poach one for you. Have some bread and jam if you are hungry."

So Frances ate bread and jam and went to school.

When the bell rang for lunch Frances sat down next to her friend Albert.

"What do you have today?" said Frances.

"I have a cream cheese-cucumber-and-tomato sandwich on rye bread," said Albert. "And a pickle to go with it. And a hard-boiled egg and a little cardboard shaker of salt to go with that. And a thermos bottle of milk. And a bunch of grapes and a tangerine. And a cup custard and a spoon to eat it with. What do you have?"

Frances opened her lunch. "Bread and jam," she said, "and milk."

"You're lucky," said Albert. "That's just what you like. You don't have to trade now."

"That's right," said Frances. "And I had bread and jam for dinner last night and for breakfast this morning."

"You certainly are lucky," said Albert.

"Yes," said Frances. "I am a very lucky girl, I guess. But I'll trade if you want to."

"That's all right," said Albert. "I *like* cream cheese with cucumbers and tomatoes on rye."

Albert took two napkins from his lunch box. He tucked one napkin under his chin. He spread the other one on his desk like a tablecloth. He arranged his lunch neatly on the napkins. With his spoon he cracked the shell of the hard-boiled egg. He peeled away the shell and bit off the end of the egg. He sprinkled salt on the yolk and set the egg down again. He unscrewed his thermos-bottle cup and filled it with milk. Then he was ready to eat his lunch. He took a bite of sandwich, a bit of pickle, a bite of hard-boiled egg, and a drink of milk. Then he sprinkled more salt on the egg and went around again. Albert made the sandwich, the pickle, the egg, and the milk come out even. He ate his bunch of grapes and his tangerine.

Then he cleared away the crumpled-up waxed paper, the eggshell, and the tangerine peel. He set the cup custard in the middle of the napkin on his desk. He took up his spoon and ate up all the custard. Then Albert folded up his napkins and put them away. He put away his cardboard saltshaker and his spoon. He screwed the cup on top of his thermos bottle. He shut his lunch box, put it back inside his desk, and sighed.

"I like to have a good lunch," said Albert.

Frances ate her bread and jam and drank her milk. Then she went out to the playground and skipped rope. She did not skip as fast as she had skipped in the morning, and she sang:

> Jam in the morning, jam at noon,
> Bread and jam by the light of the moon.
> Jam . . . is . . . very . . . nice.

When Frances got home from school, Mother said, "I know you like to have a little snack when you get home from school, and I have one all ready for you."

"I *do* like snacks!" said Frances, running to the kitchen.

"Here it is," said Mother. "A glass of milk and some nice bread and jam for you."

"Aren't you worried that maybe I will get sick and all my teeth will fall out from eating so much bread and jam?" asked Frances.

"I don't think that will happen for quite a while," said Mother. "So eat it all up and enjoy it."

Frances ate up most of her bread and jam, but she did not eat all of it. After her snack she went outside to skip rope. Frances skipped a little more slowly than she had skipped at noon, and she sang:

Jam for snacks and jam for meals,
I know how a jam jar feels—
FULL . . . OF . . . JAM!

That evening for dinner Mother cooked spaghetti and meatballs with tomato sauce.

"I am glad to see there will be enough for second helpings," said Father. "Because spaghetti and meatballs is one of my favorite dishes."

"Spaghetti and meatballs is a favorite with everybody," said Mother. "Try a little spaghetti, Gloria."

"Um," said Gloria, and tried the spaghetti.

Frances looked down at her plate and saw that there was no spaghetti and meatballs on it. There was a slice of bread and a jar of jam. Frances began to cry.

"My goodness!" said Mother. "Frances is crying!"

"What is the matter?" said Father.

Frances looked down at her plate and sang a little sad song. She sang so softly that Mother and Father could scarcely hear her:

What I am
Is tired of jam.

"I want spaghetti and meatballs," said Frances. "May I have some, please?"

"I had no idea you liked spaghetti and meatballs!" said Mother.

"How do you know what I'll like if you won't even try me?" asked Frances, wiping her eyes.

So Mother gave Frances spaghetti and meatballs, and she ate it all up.

The next day when the bell rang for lunch, Albert said, "What do you have today?"

"Well," said Frances, laying a paper doily on her desk and setting a tiny vase of violets in the middle of it, "let me see." She arranged her lunch on the doily. "I have a thermos bottle with cream of tomato soup," she said. "And a lobster-salad sandwich on thin slices of white bread. I have celery, carrot sticks, and black olives, and a little cardboard shaker of salt for the celery. And two plums and a tiny basket of cherries. And vanilla pudding with chocolate sprinkles and a spoon to eat it with."

That's a good lunch," said Albert. "I think it's nice that there are all different kinds of lunches and breakfasts and dinners and snacks.
I think eating is nice."

"So do I," said Frances, and she made the lobster-salad sandwich, the celery, and carrot sticks, and the olives come out even.

The End

Jonathan Mouse, Detective

BY INGRID OSTHEEREN

TRANSLATED BY ROSEMARY LANNING

Jonathan, the mischievous little mouse, was worried. The farm where he lived was not a happy place anymore. All the animals were miserable, and he had called a meeting to decide what to do.

"The farmer's wife has lost her golden locket," said Jonathan. "She thinks someone stole it and that's why she's in such a bad mood. She's started shouting at everyone and burning the dinner."

"She doesn't sing at milking time," murmured the cows.

"She keeps forgetting to feed me," growled Toby, the farm dog.

"She doesn't scratch me behind the ears," complained the piglet.

"Or laugh," cackled the hens.

"I've even seen her crying," said the rooster sadly.

"She's angry all the time," said the sheep. "That scares me."

"We've got to find that locket," said Jonathan. "Maybe she just mislaid it, but if it really has been stolen, we must find out who took it."

"What you need is a detective!" announced a voice from behind the bull. It was a little brown mouse.

"What is a detective?" asked Jonathan.

"Someone who catches thieves and brings back lost things," said the brown mouse. "Detectives are really clever and brave and strong. Actually, I'm a detective myself," he added proudly. "My name is Anatole and I come from the big city. I live in the walls of a detective agency, so I've been trained by the very best."

"Wonderful!" said Jonathan. "Will you help us?"

"Of course," declared Anatole. "A great detective can never resist a challenging case like this. The first thing to do is to look for clues."

Jonathan trotted along behind Anatole, who had found some hoofprints and was examining each one of them with great care.

"What I really need is a magnifying glass," muttered Anatole.

"A magnifying glass?" asked Jonathan.

"Yes, to make things look larger. Sometimes clues are very small," said Anatole.

"I think this one is very large," said Jonathan, helping the town mouse out of an especially deep hoofprint.

"You're right! This guy's enormous. It must have been him. He's big enough to climb in through the window."

"I don't think so," said Jonathan. "This hoofprint was made by the old cart horse. He can't climb at all. And he'd never squeeze through the window. Look at him!"

"Okay," said Anatole. "Cross him off the list of suspects."

"Those are pig's hoofprints," said Jonathan, peering into the rose bed.

"Then the pig did it! said Anatole. "Why else would he be lurking in the roses except to steal the locket the moment the coast was clear?"

"I don't think so," said Jonathan. "Our pig doesn't lurk. He just likes the sweet smell of flowers, especially roses."

Anatole crossed the pig off his list of suspects.

One by one, all the other animals came under suspicion.

Anatole accused the rooster of burying the locket in the compost heap, but the detective gave up his search pretty quickly when he discovered what a dirty, smelly place that was. He crossed the rooster off his list, which he studied carefully. "Aha!" he said, nodding wisely. "I should have suspected them all along."

"Let me teach you how to think like a detective," Anatole whispered to Jonathan. "I've crossed the bull and cows off the list. They could have pushed their way into the farmer's bedroom, but the staircase was too narrow. So it must have been the dog, Toby, or the cat. Toby was seen burying something in the farmyard."

Anatole persuaded Jonathan to help him find out what Toby had buried. They dug in the dirt for hours, but all they found was an old bone.

Then Anatole accused the cat. "Where were you on the night the locket disappeared?" he demanded. The cat had promised to leave the two mice in peace until they found the locket, but when Anatole accused her, she hissed and showed her claws.

"Sorry!" said Anatole hastily. "Maybe we should discuss this some other time."

Anatole pulled Jonathan aside and said in a low voice, "Well, the case is solved. You saw for yourself how she reacted; the cat must be our thief. I don't want her to know that we're on to her just yet, so I'm going to search the henhouse."

While Anatole went about his business, Jonathan sat down to think. A wisp of smoke drifted from the kitchen window, and he could hear the farmer's wife wailing that she had burned the dinner again. As he looked across the farmyard, he could see something shiny lying in the dirt. He ran over to it and discovered that it was only a shiny new coin.

"Oh well," sighed Jonathan as he looked down at the coin.

Suddenly his face lit up. "Why didn't I think of that before!" He grabbed the coin and went over to the tree where the magpie had his nest.

Just as he set the coin on the ground, a dark shadow swooped over him. "That's mine! I saw it first!" squawked the magpie.

"You did not," said Jonathan angrily. "I brought this to you as a present. You collect shiny things, don't you?"

"Yes, yes," said the magpie. "Beautiful shiny things."

"Do you have a locket?" said Jonathan.

"Is it shiny?" asked the magpie.

"Yes," said Jonathan. "It's made of gold."

"Does it have a sparkly chain?"

"It does," said Jonathan.

"Does it have a picture in the middle?" asked the magpie.

"Yes!" yelled Jonathan.

"Haven't got one of those," said the magpie as he grabbed the coin and flew to his nest. Jonathan ran after him.

"Please, Mr. Magpie!" Jonathan called up to the nest. "I know you must have the locket. You don't need it, and the farmer's wife has been miserable since that locket disappeared. Please! I'll get you an enormous piece of cheese from the larder."

"What kind of cheese?" asked the magpie.

"Any kind you want!" Jonathan replied.

And with that, the magpie finally dropped the locket.

Jonathan carefully carried the locket over to the rose bed. Then he whispered to Toby. Toby went into the kitchen and tugged at the farmer's wife's apron until she came outside.

"What do you want, you silly dog?" she said. Then she saw the locket. "Well, look at that!" cried the farmer's wife. "Good dog! You've found my locket! I must have lost it when I was cutting roses."

She patted Toby and promised him an extra-large bone.

That evening all the animals met once again behind the barn. Jonathan told them what had happened. "Now everything should get back to normal," he said. "Just wait and see. Tonight she'll be singing and laughing again."

"She thinks I found the thing," murmured Toby. "That's not fair. Jonathan was the detective after all."

"I don't mind," laughed Jonathan. "The main thing is that she's happy again."

"I wasn't much help to you either," said Anatole sadly.

"Yes you were," said Jonathan. "If you hadn't worked out who *didn't* do it, I would never have known who did."

Anatole nodded happily. "You're beginning to think like a real detective. Why don't you come back with me to the big city? We could set up our own detective agency."

"No thanks," said Jonathan. "I'm happy where I am."

Suddenly Jonathan remembered his promise to the magpie. "I've got to go!" he said as he ran off. "I have an appointment in the larder with an enormous piece of cheese!"

Mike Mulligan and His Steam Shovel

BY VIRGINIA LEE BURTON

Mike Mulligan had a steam shovel, a beautiful red steam shovel. Her name was Mary Anne. Mike Mulligan was very proud of Mary Anne. He always said that she could dig as much in a day as a hundred men could dig in a week, but he had never been quite sure that this was true.

Mike Mulligan and Mary Anne had been digging together for years and years. Mike Mulligan took such good care of Mary Anne she never grew old.

It was Mike Mulligan and Mary Anne and some others who dug the great canals for the big boats to sail through. It was Mike Mulligan and Mary Anne and some others who cut through the high mountains so that trains could go through. It was Mike Mulligan and Mary Anne and some others who lowered the hills and straightened the curves to make the long highways for the automobiles. It was Mike Mulligan and Mary Anne and some others who smoothed out the ground and filled in the holes to make the landing fields for the airplanes. And it was Mike Mulligan and Mary Anne and some others who dug the deep holes for the cellars of the tall skyscrapers in the big cities.

When people used to stop and watch them, Mike Mulligan and Mary Anne used to dig a little faster and a little better. The more people stopped, the faster and better they dug. Some days they would keep as many as thirty-seven trucks busy taking away the dirt they had dug.

Then along came the new gasoline shovels and the new electric shovels and the new Diesel motor shovels and took all the jobs away from the steam shovels. Mike Mulligan and Mary Anne were very sad.

All the other steam shovels were being sold for junk, or left out in old gravel pits to rust and fall apart. Mike loved Mary Anne. He couldn't do that to her. He had taken such good care of her that she could still dig as much in a day as a hundred men could dig in a week; at least he thought she could but he wasn't quite sure. Everywhere they went the new gas shovels and the new electric shovels and the new Diesel motor shovels had all the jobs. No one wanted Mike Mulligan and Mary Anne any more.

Then one day Mike read in a newspaper that the town of Popperville was going to build a new town hall. "We are going to dig the cellar of that town hall," said Mike to Mary Anne, and off they started.

They left the canals and the railroads and the highways and the airports and the big cities where no one wanted them any more and went away out in the country. They crawled along slowly up the hills and down the hills till they came to the little town of Popperville.

When they got there they found that the selectmen were just deciding who should dig the cellar for the new town hall. Mike Mulligan spoke to Henry B. Swap, one of the selectman.

"I heard," he said, "that you are going to build a new town hall. Mary Anne and I will dig the cellar for you in just one day."

"What!" said Henry B. Swap. "Dig a cellar in a day! It would take a hundred men at least a week to dig the cellar for our new town hall."

"Sure," said Mike, "but Mary Anne can dig as much in a day as a hundred men can dig in a week." Though he had never been quite sure that this was true. Then he added, "If we can't do it, you won't have to pay."

Henry B. Swap thought that this would be an easy way to get part of the cellar dug for nothing, so he smiled in rather a mean way and gave the job of digging the cellar of the new town hall to Mike Mulligan and Mary Anne.

They started in early the next morning just as the sun was coming up. Soon a little boy came along. "Do you think you will finish by sundown?" he said to Mike Mulligan.

"Sure," said Mike, "if you stay and watch us. We always work faster and better when someone is watching us." So the little boy stayed to watch.

Then Mrs. McGillicuddy, Henry B. Swap, and the Town Constable came over to see what was happening, and they stayed to watch. Mike Mulligan and Mary Anne dug a little faster and a little better.

This gave the little boy a good idea. He ran off and told the postman with the morning mail, the telegraph boy on his bicycle, the milkman with his cart and horse, the doctor on his way home, and the farmer and his family coming into town for the day, and they all stopped and stayed to watch. That made Mike Mulligan and Mary Anne dig a little faster and a little better.

They finished the first corner neat and square . . . but the sun was getting higher.

Clang! Clang! Clang! The Fire Department arrived. They had seen the smoke and thought there was a fire. Then the little boy said, "Why don't you stay and watch?"

So the Fire Department of Popperville stayed to watch Mike Mulligan and Mary Anne. When they heard the fire engine, the children in the school across the street couldn't keep their eyes on their lessons. The teacher called a long recess and the whole school came out to watch. That made Mike Mulligan and Mary Anne dig still faster and still better.

They finished the second corner neat and square, but the sun was right up in the top of the sky.

Now the girl who answers the telephone called up the next towns of Bangerville and Bopperville and Kipperville and Kopperville and told them what was happening in Popperville. All the people came over to see if Mike Mulligan and his steam shovel could dig the cellar in just one day. The more people came, the faster Mike Mulligan and Mary Anne dug. But they would have to hurry. They were only halfway through and the sun was beginning to go down.

They finished the third corner . . . neat and square.

Never had Mike Mulligan and Mary Anne had so many people to watch them; never had they dug so fast and so well; and never had the sun seemed to go down so fast.

"Hurry, Mike Mulligan! Hurry! Hurry!" shouted the little boy. "There's not much more time!"

Dirt was flying everywhere, and the smoke and steam were so thick that the people could hardly see anything. But listen! Bing! Bang! Crash! Slam! Louder and Louder, Faster and Faster.

Then suddenly it was quiet. Slowly the dirt settled down. The smoke and steam cleared away, and there was the cellar all finished.

Four corners . . . neat and square; four walls . . . straight down, and Mike Mulligan and Mary Anne at the bottom, and the sun was just going down behind the hill.

"Hurray!" shouted the people. "Hurray for Mike Mulligan and his steam shovel! They have dug the cellar in just one day."

Suddenly the little boy said, "How are they going to get out?"

"That's right," said Mrs. McGillicuddy to Henry B. Swap. "How is he going to get his steam shovel out?" Henry B. Swap didn't answer, but he smiled in rather a mean way.

Then everybody said, "How are they going to get out? 'Hi! Mike Mulligan! How are you going to get your steam shovel out?'"

Mike Mulligan looked around at the four square walls and four square corners, and he said, "We've dug so fast and we've dug so well that we've quite forgotten to leave a way out!"

Nothing like this had ever happened to Mike Mulligan and Mary Anne before and they didn't know what to do. Nothing like this had ever happened before in Popperville. Everybody started talking at once, and everybody had a different idea, and everybody thought that his idea was the best. They talked and they talked and they argued and they fought till they were worn out, and still no one knew how to get Mike Mulligan and Mary Anne out of the cellar they had dug.

Then Henry B. Swap said, "The job isn't finished because Mary Anne isn't out of the cellar, so Mike Mulligan won't get paid." And he smiled again in a rather mean way.

Now the little boy, who had been keeping very quiet, had another good idea. He said, "Why couldn't we leave Mary Anne in the cellar and build the new town hall above her? Let her be the furnace for the new town hall and let Mike Mulligan be the janitor. Then you wouldn't have to buy a new furnace, and we could pay Mike Mulligan for digging the cellar in just one day."

"Why not?" said Henry B. Swap, and smiled in a way that was not quite so mean.

"Why not?" said Mrs. McGillicuddy.

"Why not?" said the Town Constable.

"Why not?" said all the people.

So they found a ladder and climbed down into the cellar to ask Mike Mulligan and Mary Anne.

"Why not?" said Mike Mulligan.

So it was decided and everybody was happy. They built the new town hall right over Mike Mulligan and Mary Anne. It was finished before winter.

Every day the little boy goes over to see Mike Mulligan and Mary Anne, and Mrs. McGillicuddy takes him nice hot apple pies. As for Henry B. Swap, he spends most of his time in the cellar of the new town hall listening to the stories that Mike Mulligan has to tell and smiling in a way that isn't mean at all.

Now when you go to Popperville, be sure to go down in the cellar of the new town hall. There they'll be, Mike Mulligan and Mary Anne. Mike in his rocking chair and Mary Anne beside him, warming up the meetings in the new town hall.

Boy Invents Toys!

Richie Stachowski's wet and wild inventions are making waves in toy stores.

Richie Stachowski, 14, got a big idea while snorkeling in Hawaii with his dad four years ago.

"I was seeing cool things like weird angelfish, turtles, and eels," Richie remembers. He wanted to point the critters out to his dad before they swam away. But going to the surface to talk was way too slow.

At the surface, Richie asked his dad if there was a way to talk underwater. When his dad said no, Richie decided to invent an underwater walkie-talkie.

He made a few sketches in the family's hotel room that night. Then, when his family got home to California, Richie researched how sound travels underwater. He began experimenting with everything from soda cans to rolled-up sheets of plastic. He used $267 he had in a savings account to buy supplies.

Some parents would not be happy if their kid emptied out a savings account to fiddle around with cans under water. But Richie's mom, Barbara, is an inventor too. "We thought Richie's product would be really successful," she says.

Richie tried out about 100 different designs for his underwater walkie-talkie. His dad helped him test them in neighborhood swimming pools. After about three weeks of hard work, Richie finally had a design that allowed two people 15 feet apart to talk underwater.

Now Richie was ready to sell his *Water Talkies.* But how? "We went out and looked at different stores," Barbara remembers. "We picked five or six that we liked. We started at one store because it was Richie's favorite."

Richie looked up the phone number of the buyer—the person who chooses the toys and games the store will sell—in one of his mom's reference books on inventing. His name was Chuck Miller. Richie called Miller to ask for a meeting. Was he scared? "I was only 10," Richie says. "I was too young to be scared."

Miller was impressed. Pool and water toys, he explained, are pretty much the same year after year— rafts, floats, beach balls. "Richie had something that was different," says Miller, "so I jumped at the chance." He invited Richie and his mom to the store's headquarters in New Jersey to tell him more about *Water Talkies.*

"I gave the sales speech," Richie remembers. He showed off his package design, discussed prices and other details, and explained when he could deliver the toys. The wheeling and dealing went on for 2 1/2 hours.

Near the end of the meeting, Richie showed Miller a fish tank with a *Water Talkie* inserted in one side. Richie talked through the *Water Talkie* while Miller listened through a stethoscope pressed to the glass. "Can you hear me?"

Richie asked. Miller said, "Whoa, this is great!" When the dealing was over, he placed an order for 50,000 sets of *Water Talkies.*

Back at home, Richie hired a business man to find a factory to make the toys and help run his new company. Meanwhile, Richie drummed up more sales. And while kids across the country were discovering *Water Talkies* during the summer of 1997, Richie came up with two new toys. The following year, he brought out the Aqua Scope (a pool periscope) and the *Bumper Jumper Water Pumper* (a float with a water-blasting paddle).

Recently Richie decided to sell his toy business so he could focus on school and sports. He wouldn't tell us exactly how much money his inventions brought him, but said *almost* all of it is earning interest in the bank. He added that he spent $400 and gave $1,000 to charities that support kid entrepreneurs. "I don't need the money now," he explains. Plus, he says, he's not in it for the money. He just loves to invent!

Stone Soda Bread

BY JULIE DOUGLAS

You see, it all started when a stranger came strolling up the road from Ballyknuckles. He seemed a friendly sort, but they weren't used to strange faces in the village. He called himself Rafferty. He was on his way7 to the big town, so he said, and was looking for a bite to eat.

The menfolk mumbled, "We've nothing to share."

The women agreed, "Not a scrap to spare."

"No matter," Rafferty chuckled. "Lucky for me I know the recipe for stone soda bread. Made with only a stone, so it is."

Mrs. O'Mara was the first to speak. "Soda bread from a stone?" she clucked. "Why, what nonsense!" She wrung her apron in her pudgy hands and rolled her eyes at the stranger.

"No, it's true," Rafferty exclaimed. "I learned the recipe from my own granny when I was but a lad." He pulled a stone the size of hen's egg from his pocket.

"Ah, this will do quite nicely," he cooed, rubbing the stone on his shirtsleeve. The villagers gathered in closer. Could it be true? Bread from a stone?

"Do you say a magic spell now?" little Liam asked.

"A spell, is it? Oh goodness, no, child," said the stranger. "No, all I'll need is this stone . . . and the recipe, of course." He tapped his head and winked at the boy.

"Is it tasty, then?" asked Mrs. O'Mara, her tummy rumbling.

"Ah, yes, indeed," said Rafferty dreamily. "It's best warm out of the oven—all crusty and chewy at the same time." He licked his lips. "I'd better get started then."

"Can we help?" Liam offered. After all, it is not every day you see a loaf of bread made from only a stone.

"Yes, yes," the villagers agreed, for though they weren't willing to share their dinners, they weren't opposed to a bit of work. The stranger scratched his head.

"I can't say that I've ever had help with the recipe," he said, shaking his head. The villagers looked at him sadly. "Still, it couldn't hurt, could it?" A cheer went up, and then they listened carefully to what he told them.

"First, we will need a bowl and a spoon," he began.

Mrs. Finnegan clapped her hands. "I have just the thing," she cried.

"Yes, grand," Rafferty said when she returned. He dropped the stone into the bowl and began to stir. He whistled a little jig as he worked.

"That's it?" asked Liam. "That's all you do?"

Rafferty handed Liam the bowl. "It takes a bit of stirring, lad," he said. "Would you be so kind?"

Liam eagerly took the spoon and began to stir with all his might.

"That's all there is to it," Rafferty announced. The villagers stared in disbelief.

"Of course, this is just the basic recipe," he said. "To make a really fine stone soda bread, it's nice to add a little flour and baking soda."

"I have flour," shouted an old woman. She hobbled off and returned with a sack of flour and a spoonful of baking soda. Before he scooped the flour into the bowl, Rafferty took out the stone.

"It's best to put the stone in last . . . if you are going to be adding other ingredients, that is," he said.

"Other ingredients?" said Liam.

"Well, it's not completely necessary," Rafferty said, "but some sugar and an egg would be nice." Before you could say Killybegs, the shopkeeper had returned with a cup of sugar and a fine, brown egg.

"The very thing," said Rafferty.

Liam stirred the flour, soda, sugar, and egg. "Should we add the stone now?" he asked.

"Well, I suppose we could," Rafferty said, "if we are not going to add anything else."

"What else?" the villagers cried.

"Oh, perhaps a little oil and splash of buttermilk," he said, "but only if you think we need them."

The villagers answered by running to fetch the oil and buttermilk. Mr. Powers even brought a sack of raisins to add to the mix. Liam stirred and stirred as they added the new ingredients.

Rafferty poked his finger into the batter and took a taste. "H'm," he sighed. "I daresay that this is *almost* the best stone soda bread I've ever made."

"Almost the best!" cried Father Walsh. "Tell us, what would make it better?"

"Well, if I had some caraway seeds to add . . ." he began.

"I'm your man," cried Father, and he raced to the rectory to collect the seeds.

Liam stirred the mixture until it was thick and sticky. Rafferty poured the batter into a loaf pan. Then, with the flick of his wrist, he cut a cross in the top of the loaf.

The villagers crowded into Mrs. O'Mara's kitchen as she popped the pan into the oven. Soon a delicious smell wrapped around the hungry villagers.

"But Mr. Rafferty," Liam whispered, "the stone! We forgot to add the stone."

Rafferty smiled at Liam. "The bread is actually better when you keep the stone in your pocket," he told the boy.

Liam held the stone tightly in his hand and blinked at Rafferty.

"Besides," Rafferty said, "I'm passing the recipe on to you, lad. You'll need a fine stone like that for the next batch."

When the bread was done, Rafferty placed it on the table. He smiled at the villagers. "Of course, you know what would really make this stone soda bread perfect?" he asked.

"A pot of tea and some fresh butter, perhaps?" suggested Mrs. O'Mara. She put a kettle on to boil as Rafferty sliced the bread.

"And stew!" Cried Mrs. Finnegan as she lugged a steaming kettle through the door of the cottage. She ladled up bowls of it for everyone.

Soon the stranger and the villagers were feasting. Laughter and singing filled Mrs. O'Mara's cottage.

"Tis the best stone soda bread I've ever tasted," exclaimed Rafferty as he winked at Liam.

"Tis!" agreed the villagers.

And to think—it was made with nothing but a stone.